The Backyard Money Machine:

How to organize and operate a successful Garage Sale

By L. R. Schmeltz

Silver Streak **Publications**

Bettendorf, IA

The Backyard Money Machine:
How to organize and operate a successful Garage Sale

By Les R. Schmeltz
Illustrations by Joe Getz & Becky Holdorf

Published by:
Silver Streak Publications
1823 Sussex Court
Bettendorf, IA 52722

Printed in the United States of America

Publisher's Cataloging in Publication
(Prepared by Quality Books, Inc.)

Schmeltz, Leslie R., 1943-
  The backyard money machine: how to organize and operate a successful garage sale/ Les R. Schmeltz.
    p. cm.
  Includes biographical references and index.
  ISBN 0-9635321-0-3

  1. Garage sales.   I. Title.

HF5482.3.S36 1993   658.8'7
                                            QBI92-2798

TABLE OF CONTENTS

TABLE OF CONTENTS

Warning--Disclaimer

Acknowledgments

Probably the most important contributors to this book are the thousands of people whose garage sales we visited. Each of them supplied ideas that are, in some fashion, included in this book. The shoppers at our own sales also contributed many insights into the behaviors and attitudes listed herein.

Many thanks to Joe Getz for his imaginative illustrations for the cover and chapter heads, Becky Holdorf for her expert assistance with the cover and appendices, Bob Hanson and Carol Swift for their proofreading skills and helpful suggestions, Bruce Pogue for his computer expertise and Sue Meyers for much helpful advice.

Finally, thanks to my wife and business partner, Diane for her patient understanding and encouragement during the long hours of research and preparation of this book.

> **"Opportunity is missed by most people because it is dressed in overalls and looks like work"**
>
> ....*Thomas Alva Edison*

The spirit of the American entrepreneur is alive and well! In its' most basic form, this spirit surfaces in the hearts and minds of those who spend hours sorting, cleaning, displaying and selling unwanted possessions and other homespun merchandise to their friends and neighbors. On any given weekend there are literally thousands of garage, tag, craft, rummage, household, moving, divorce, farm, etc. sales. The driving force behind each of these sales is a group of entrepreneurs who hope to transform their merchandise into a significant amount of cash. As a matter of fact, the whole idea behind garage sales if to provide an opportunity for shoppers to exchange their cash for your goods.

Millions of shoppers travel from sale to sale in search of bargains and end up spending billions of dollars. In fact, the Wall Street Journal has estimated the annual yield from garage sales at approximately 2 billion dollars. When craft sales, bazaars, estate and other personal sales are added in, the figure could easily reach several times that amount

WHAT ARE GARAGE SALES?

In this book we will use the term "garage sale" to include most of the types of sales listed above. Although they are known by different names, most of these sales feature similar merchandise and a striking resemblance in set-up and operation. More often than not, the name for a sale is derived from the location, (garage, patio, yard), group participating (neighborhood, multi-family, social group), circumstances surrounding the sale (moving, estate, divorce), or specific type of merchandise (bake, craft, book).

Concept Of Personal Merchandise

Most of the merchandise sold at garage sales is either homemade or used. We have seen a wide variety of items ranging from brand new unwanted gifts (still sealed in their packages) to things that look like they should have been thrown in the trash a long time ago. The merchandise is personal in that it has been owned by someone else prior to being offered for sale.

Actually Short Lived Businesses

Garage sales differ from retail businesses in two important respects--lack of standard prices and a finite period of operation. The majority of items are long past the "manufacturers suggested list price" in both age and condition, so pricing becomes primarily a matter of agreement between buyer and seller. Prices tend to become much more flexible as the end of the sale approaches--a fact that is very well known by garage sale shoppers. Since sales are almost always relatively short, there is added pressure on the seller to clear out most of the inventory by the end of the specified time.

WHY PEOPLE HOLD SALES

Of all the things that motivate people to hold a garage sale, raising cash is the common denominator. While it may be fashionable to insist that other reasons are more important, the prospect of raising a significant amount of cash by using your brain and some elbow grease but almost no new capital has much appeal.

The amount of cash raised from a well planned and executed sale can be considerable. Most sale holders report earning several hundred dollars, others routinely raise thousands. On the other hand, those who are unwilling to devote the time and effort to properly plan and execute their sale are often disappointed at the trivial amount of money they raise. As we will see repeatedly throughout this book, the difference between just doing the job and doing the job right translates into a great deal of money.

It makes sense to sell your unwanted household or other merchandise rather than just discarding it. Of course, the garage sale is often used as an intermediate stop between the house and garbage dump. We will be outlining many ambitious steps to help sellers raise more cash, but you will need more than potential garbage to sell.

A garage sale can be a lot of fun, especially if friends and neighbors get involved. People working toward a common goal enjoy a special type of bond. It's amazing how much people enjoy the challenge of making a sale more successful and selling some of their tackiest items. Adding to the fun, of course, are the "people watching" and socializing with all your customers.

> *"It's just like having
> a license to
> print your own money"
> .....Lord Thomson of Fleet,
> 1894-1977*

WHY PEOPLE SHOP SALES

Garage sale customers are among the most thrifty to be found. Although there is great diversity in almost every other area, garage sale shoppers share one common characteristic--**they are looking for merchandise they want to buy at a price they want (or can afford) to pay.** Stretching the dollar is no idle expression when it comes to these shoppers!

Some folks shop garage sales in order to satisfy a desire to own things from the past. The nostalgia motive can be very powerful and works to the advantage of the seller, if handled properly. For those interested in more than just a casual piece or two of nostalgia, garage sales provide the perfect opportunity to add to collections at a reasonable price. In fact, collectors are among the most avid garage sale shoppers.

Professional antique and collectible dealers are usually among the first to appear at a sale and buy merchandise at wholesale levels whenever possible. Those planning a garage sale of their own in the near future are looking for bargains and specific items to round out their inventory.

Garage sale shopping can be fun. The prospect of getting a bargain or just spending a Saturday morning socializing at various sales in town motivates many a shopper to hit the "sale trail."

> *"There's many a good tune played on an old fiddle"*
> *.....Samuel Butler 1835-1902*

PURPOSE OF THIS BOOK

This book is designed to help the seller make the most of a garage sale opportunity. Sellers really don't need to hear about the legendary bargains we've all found at garage sales. Instead they need ideas to help make their sale the most profitable they've every had. A successful sale requires a considerable amount of planning and hard work, but can be an immensely satisfying venture when completed.

Throughout this book, we will provide a lot of ideas for the planning and execution of a garage sale. All the ideas presented have worked for someone else, many are just plain common sense. It is not necessary for you to use every idea to have a successful sale, just those that will be of some help to you.

Some basic facts that will be needed to begin planning your sale will be discussed in the early chapters. While we will confine our discussion to garage sales at first, later chapters will focus on organizational details for other types of sales.

Merchandise selection, pricing and display are critical to the success of any sale. Since the range of items is likely to be extremely wide, we will offer suggestions that pertain to the most common types of items found at garage sales. We will offer

> *"The reward of a thing
> well done,
> is to have done it"*
> *.....R.W. Emerson, 1803-1882*

some ideas for merchandise that can, with very little additional capital, significantly increase the profitability of a sale.

The best organized sale in the world is doomed to failure unless potential shoppers are aware of its existence. Advertising and publicity are critical in determining the overall success or failure of a sale. Signs, newspaper advertisements, and other ways to inform the public should be cost effective and efficient. We will offer many suggestions for making the most of your advertising budget and coordinating efforts to bring shoppers "through the door."

Once shoppers have been attracted to a well-organized sale, the mechanics of conducting the sale can have a profound influence on whether or not they buy any merchandise. It is not unusual to hear shoppers complain about treatment they have received at garage sales. No matter how interesting the merchandise or reasonable the prices, shoppers just will not buy when they feel they have been treated rudely or looked down upon. Competition is stiff when there is a garage sale on just about every corner during the summer months. Sellers must learn the secrets of conducting a sale in such a way that shoppers will want to buy and encourage their friends to do the same.

> "*A man must make his*
> *opportunity,*
> *as oft as find it*"
> .....*Francis Bacon, 1561-1626*

Having a solid plan to work from at every stage of a sale can go a long way in reducing the stress that accompanies any major project. Knowing that you are prepared when the first wave of shoppers arrives at your door can transform a potentially stressful situation into one where the results of your planning come shining through. While minor problems may surface during the planning and execution of any sale, we will do our best to see that those problems remain minor annoyances, not major crises.

In a nutshell, the purpose of this book is to provide you with the tools to help do the job right. While it is true that anyone can put together a garage sale and make a little money, those willing to spend the time and effort to follow the suggestions outlined in this book will be able to put together a garage sale and make a LOT OF MONEY.

ORGANIZATION OF THIS BOOK

This book is designed to address the six basic areas of any endeavor--**why, who, when, where, what** and **how**. The first chapter will provide information on why to have a sale, who will sell and the best times to plan a garage sale. Location considerations will be covered in chapter two and merchandise will be covered in the next two chapters. Most of the rest of the book will be devoted to the area of HOW. How to plan, how to

> *"Genius is one percent inspiration, ninety nine percent perspiration"*
> *...Thomas Edison, 1847-1931*

advertise, how to most effectively display your merchandise, how to conduct your sale, how to protect yourself and how to close the sale.

Specific chapter titles are as follows:

1. Why, Who And When

2. Where To Hold Sales

3. What To Sell

4. Antiques and Collectibles

5. Planning Your Sale

6. Informing Everyone

7. Displaying Your Merchandise

8. Conducting Your Sale

9. Common Sense Crime Prevention

10. After The Sale

11. Special Situation Sales

In the Appendices you will find checklists to help organize every phase of your sale. Samples of signs, promotional materials and other things necessary to actually conduct a sale are included in the next section. Finally, a list of pricing guides and sources of additional information will help answer any specific questions you may have.

Specific Appendix titles:

A.   Checklists

B.   Signs And Samples

C.   Pricing Guides And Sources Of Information

WHY TO HOLD A SALE

In this section, we will attempt to outline the reasons most people offer for holding a garage sale.

Raise Cash

The amount of cash raised depends on two factors--the inventory you have to sell and the amount of work you are willing to devote to advertising, display and conducting your sale.

People are often amazed at the amount of money to be made by selling relatively inexpensive items. Sales can raise anywhere from a less than a hundred to well over a thousand dollars a day. As we noted in the introduction, the purpose of this book is to help you, the seller, increase the amount of cash raised from your garage sales. While there are no guarantees, each of the suggestions offered in this book represent proven methods that have helped others. The degree to which you apply these ideas will have a definite impact on the overall profit figures for your sale.

Sell Merchandise

Once you have made the decision to hold a sale rather than just discard or donate merchandise, the items in question become simply a vehicle for

> *"Money is like a sixth sense without which you cannot make use of the other five."*
> *...W. Somerset Maugham,*
> *1874-1965*

raising cash. You are placed in the same position as any other business person and must make decisions regarding your sale while viewing it as a short term business that you want to be as profitable as possible. Shoppers are more than willing to buy items they can use for a fraction of the new cost, so everyone benefits from garage sales.

Your merchandise will consist of unwanted items that you find around the house, marginally wanted items that you would like to convert to cash and special merchandise obtained for the garage sale. All of us have a few things around the house that we would be willing to sell if the price was right. As we will see in a later chapter, these items can be used to increase the amount of merchandise displayed. Whether they are sold or n)t, these types of items can play an important role in attracting people to your sale.

Moving

Those about to move have good reasons to hold a garage sale. Often the price to move an item (particularly one that is heavy or bulky) may nearly equal the price of replacing that item. There are things that just won't fit in to the new home and must be replaced--so why move them? Moving provides the perfect opportunity to get rid of some items that you are just sick and tired of seeing. The extra cash from a garage sale will help with replacement expenses.

Special Situations

Most garage sales are organized and operated by a single family or group of families for the purpose of selling their unwanted surplus. Some situations call for a similar sale, but with important differences.

Estate Sales

Estate sales are essentially garage sales with some difficult emotions attached. Those charged with the disposition of household and personal effects from an estate are under considerable stress and will certainly benefit from some of the procedures outlined in this book. Since the assets of an estate must often be divided (usually without agreement as to who gets how much), it is important to raise as much cash as possible while liquidating the entire estate.

Worthy Cause Sales

"Worthy Cause" sales are designed to raise funds for a charity or social group. Often, these take the form of group garage sales with varying degrees of success. We will discuss these sales at some length in a later chapter and offer some suggestions on how to raise more money.

WHO WILL SELL

In its simplest form, a garage sale is run by an individual or single family and features merchandise belonging exclusively to that family. Rarely do things stay that simple, however. Once neighbors and friends learn of the sale, they always have "just a few things" they'd like to sell.

> *"Everybody wants to*
> *get inta the act!"*
> *...Jimmy Durante, 1893-1980*

Multiple Families

The next step, of course, is to include merchandise from several families. Actually, the multi-family sale has some advantages:

1. Many shoppers feel a multi-family sale offers a lot of extra merchandise.

2. Advertising costs and the workload of setting up a sale can be distributed among more people.

3. There is a possibility of choosing the best sale location.

4. An opportunity is provided for the families to spend some time together.

The big attraction of a multi-family sale for the shopper is a lot of extra merchandise. Be cautious, however, since regular garage sale shoppers tend to avoid multi-family sales because the merchandise often turns out to be nothing but a collection of everyone's junk!

Neighborhoods

Residents of neighborhoods, apartment complexes and mobile home parks often band together and sponsor group sales. The prospect of being able to attend a heavy concentration of sales in a relatively small area has tremendous appeal to garage sale shoppers. Several neighborhoods in our area report excellent results from their annual sale. College dormitories have sponsored "clearance sales" at the end of the school year and reported similar success. In this type of arrangement, everyone holds their own sale and shares the advertising and promotional expenses.

Often neighborhood sales include a refreshment area operated by the neighbors or some charitable organization. Anything that can get shoppers to linger increases the chances of selling more merchandise.

The organizers of the sale must plan carefully to make sure that:

1. Efforts are coordinated.

2. Everyone who wants to participate is included.

3. Mutual problems such as traffic control and parking are handled efficiently.

Consignment

Consignment sales are quite different from the group sales outlined so far in that one individual or family solicits merchandise from several sources and charges a fee for selling each item. Those furnishing consignment merchandise do not usually want to be personally involved in the sale.

Consignment arrangements offer a good way to expand the selection of merchandise available at a sale. More people (including the consignors) will be interested and may help attract shoppers to your sale. The commissions you earn will help increase the amount of money you make from the sale. Generally you should expect to charge a commission rate of 20-25%, slightly less if the consignor is willing to help conduct the sale.

There are disadvantages to consignment arrangements. You may not want to be responsible for items belonging to others or the record keeping necessary to document sales. You could be held responsible for items that are damaged or stolen. There is always the potential for misunderstanding unless the terms of your arrangement are written and clearly understood in advance.

If you feel the merchandise being offered on consignment will not be an asset to your sale, there is no reason that you must accept it. Be selective and include **only** those items you know will sell and help sell the other items in your sale.

Kids

Should kids be included in your garage sale plans? It depends on their age and abilities. Preschoolers will not be much help and may resent the extra time you are taking to organize and conduct the sale. If your kids are old enough, they can help find unwanted items for the sale. Kids who are school age can set up a booth and be responsible for their own merchandise or sell refreshments. Teenagers may want to set up their own separate area and feature merchandise of interest to their own age group. By participating in your garage sale, your children will learn a lot about the real world of merchandise and money.

Groups And "Worthy Cause" Sales

Many groups have discovered that garage sales can be an excellent way to raise funds. Unfortunately, group sales are often avoided by garage sale shoppers because the quality of merchandise donated is usually poor or the prices are unreasonable. Members of the group involved are often the prime customers as well as merchandise suppliers to these sales.

WHO WILL BUY

Usually, the first customers at any garage sale are relatives, friends and neighbors of those conducting the sale. These customers will be excellent "bellwethers" and not hesitate, if asked, to offer suggestions on how to improve various aspects of your sale.

Garage Sale Regulars

There are several identifiable groups of regular garage sale shoppers. The regulars are among the most dollar-wise shoppers you will ever come across. They **KNOW** their prices and will simply not buy if prices are too high. On the other hand, they are likely to buy just about anything if the price is right--even if they really have no need for the item!

Professional Fleas And Dealers

Professional fleas and dealers in antiques, used furniture, coins and collectibles frequently travel the garage sale circuit. These people shop for specific merchandise and buy only if the price is right. Price bargaining is part of their style. They are tough buyers who know an unrecognized treasure when they see it. Rarely will the professionals identify themselves unless it is to their advantage in price negotiations.

Bargain Hunters

Bargain Hunters are people looking for specific items for which they have immediate use. They usually have limited funds and are very careful shoppers. Bargain Hunters will ask about specific merchandise if it is not displayed and bargain for better prices on things they find.

Junk Addicts

Junk Addicts are the most fun shoppers to watch. They are fascinated with junk and will buy most anything that strikes their fancy. Price is not a big consideration to this type of shopper. Quite often the Junk Addict will have no real use for the merchandise other than the potential of it "coming in handy sometime."

Collectors

Collectors are frequent garage sale shoppers and **very** selective in their purchases. They are looking to add to their collection at bargain prices. Collectors will **not** pay retail prices for any collectible they buy at a garage sale. Attracting collectors can be as simple as mentioning their

> *"Here's the rule for bargains:*
> *Do other men,*
> *for they would do you.*
> *That's the true*
> *business precept"*
> *.....Charles Dickens, 1812-1870*

specific interest items in your newspaper advertising.

Garage Sale Planners

Those planning their own sale are often avid garage sale shoppers. In addition to looking for good ideas, these folks often buy bargain priced merchandise to resell. These shoppers will sometimes offer to buy the remaining inventory at the end of a sale.

Impulse Shoppers

Impulse shoppers usually stop at a garage sale as the result of seeing a sign that attracted their attention. Rarely do they respond to newspaper advertising. They enjoy seeing what is featured at the sale and comparing prices with other sales they've seen.

Price, however, is not the primary determiner of whether or not you will sell the impulse shopper. Just as the decision to stop at a sale was made impulsively, buying a specific piece of merchandise is done in the same way. If an item strikes their fancy, impulse shoppers will pay almost any price.

Lookers

Any sale will attract a large group of lookers. Their primary reason for attending the sale is curiosity. They love to look around and socialize. Often the lookers are bored and go to sales mostly because they don't have much else too do. They really don't know what they want or need, consequently they rarely buy much of anything.

Lookers can be an asset to your sale in two ways, however. Potential shoppers like to see other people at a sale before they stop and lookers may help attract these shoppers. Quite often lookers know of someone looking for specific items and may help spread the word about your sale.

A Few Last Thoughts About Shoppers

Many garage sale shoppers do not fit in to the stereotypes listed above. We've seen young and old, single, married and family groups, friends, relatives and neighbors at many sales. There are newlyweds looking to equip their first home; expectant parents shopping for baby items; families looking for children's toys, clothes and furniture; folks on fixed incomes buying necessities; and other shoppers looking for any number of things.

You'll see shoppers driving everything from clunkers to Cadillacs. They'll pay for purchases from bags of coins or rolls of hundred dollar bills. One of the most interesting aspects of garage sales is "people watching" all the folks who stop in to shop. Although there is great diversity in almost every other area, garage sale shoppers share one common characteristic--they are looking for merchandise they want to buy at a price they want (or can afford) to pay.

WHEN TO HAVE A SALE

The proper timing for your sale is extremely important. Consider the following factors in deciding just the right time for your sale:

Seasons

Certain months are excellent for garage sales and some months should be avoided. November and December, for instance, are likely to find potential shoppers more concerned with holiday gifts than garage sales. August is a prime vacation month in many areas. In the Midwest, January and February are horrible weather months, as are June and July in tropical climates.

The time of the month can make a big difference in the potential success of your sale. Most people get paid near the end of the month, so a sale held around the first will find people with more money available to shop.

Consider the prime sale season in your area. There is something of a shopping mall effect among garage sale shoppers--that is, more sales will generate more buyer traffic and enthusiasm. During the prime sale season, shoppers will spend the day "hitting sales" all over town. If you want to be one of the crowd, hold your sale in prime time. While there are advantages to holding sales in pleasant weather, those held in the off season often get extra attention from serious shoppers. If you have a good variety of items to sell and feel your sale would be better on it's own, try planning it for the off season.

You also need to consider the nature of the majority of items you expect to sell. If you plan to feature spring and summer clothing, the ideal time for your sale would be early in the spring.

Everyone else in town will be trying to sell winter clothes in the spring, but who wants to buy things they won't be able to use for almost a full year? Similarly, late summer is the best time to dispose of fall and winter clothes. If your other items are not particularly time dependent, consider holding your sale very early in the season for most of the clothes you expect to sell.

Consult a community calendar and schedule your sale so it will not conflict with major events. While some community events bring in large crowds, rarely are garage sales successful when planned in conjunction with those events. Of course, flea markets or house tours are obvious exceptions.

Holidays are rarely ideal times for garage sales. Craft sales, however, are often timed to coincide with the shopping period for major holidays. Early summer is an excellent time for Mother's and Father's days, early November for Christmas, etc. Most craft item purchases are impulsive in nature and far less price dependent than other types of merchandise.

Bake sales also tend to do very well just before major holidays, particularly if they feature seasonal items--pumpkin pies for Thanksgiving, decorated cookies for Christmas, etc.

There are numerous times of the year to promote specific items. Take a clue from retailers as they promote office supplies around tax time, picnic supplies around the 4th of July, clothes for back to school, etc. You can advertise a "Back To School" or "Summer Clothes Galore" garage sale!

Days And Hours

Most garage sales run two or three days, although sales can run anywhere from one day to a week. One day sales are great IF they are exceptionally well organized, have readily salable merchandise and are advertised heavily. Week-long sales should be considered only if there is a LOT of uncommonly interesting merchandise and advertising. There are two major factors to consider when setting the length of a sale--the amount of merchandise and the amount of advertising you are willing to do. We will discuss both factors in subsequent chapters.

Regardless of the length of your sale, consider carefully the day(s) of the week and hours your sale will be held. In our area, most garage sales are held on Thursday, Friday and Saturday although some start on Wednesday or end on Sunday. One day sales are usually held on Friday or Saturday. Craft and specialty sales are most often held on the weekends.

Hours of operation depend largely on the type of customers you hope to attract. You will find that many customers like to get to garage sales early while there are still bargains to be had, so for those folks you will need to open quite early. Others will not be able to shop until later in the day. It is important that you allow enough time for both working and non-working customers to attend your sale. Usually that means at least day of the weekend and extended hours of operation.

Think of your own shopping habits--would you be able to shop if your favorite stores were open only a few hours a day? Most retailers gear their hours so that evenings and weekends are available for those who prefer to shop at those times. It would definitely be to your advantage to start early or stay open late enough to allow everyone interested in attending your sale to do so.

Consider holding your sale during off-beat days or hours such as a "Monday Moonlight Sale" from 5-10 PM, particularly if many of your items will appeal to folks who would be working during more orthodox sale hours.

If you would like to guarantee a crowd, advertise an "Early Bird Sale," open at 6 AM and offer FREE coffee and donuts from 6 to 9 AM. Buy a few dozen donuts, make a large urn of coffee and get ready for a pleasant surprise. Serious shoppers will go almost anywhere for something free, so your sale will attract the people who may prove to be your best customers. Since they'll have to wait for other sales in the area to open, they will spend more time looking at your merchandise. If your prices are reasonable and your merchandise well displayed, you may have to close early due to lack of remaining inventory!

> *"Well, it only proves what they always say--give the public something they want to see and they'll come out for it."*
> *...Red Skelton, 1911-*

As a rule of thumb, begin your sale by 8 AM and close no earlier than 5 PM. It is VERY important that your sale be in operation during the advertised hours. It may be tempting to open late or close early, but you could miss the one or two shoppers who may have been your best customers.

Early Birds

No matter what time you decide to open your sale, there will always be one or two "Early Birds" who show up earlier. Quite often they will offer some excuse for not being able to shop during your advertised hours and will disrupt your last minute preparations. On the other hand, we have had early shoppers buy a lot of merchandise at some of our sales. Most garage sale organizers insist that EVERYONE wait until the sale is open before allowing them to shop.

IMPORTANCE OF LOCATION

Real estate professionals say there are three things to consider when shopping for a home-- location, location and location! Retail merchants use elaborate market research techniques to find just the right location for their business. Garage sales, on the other hand, are often held in some very inopportune places. Although you may not have much choice in locating your sale, consider the following factors IF you do have any choice at all:

1. The **location** selected should be suitable for a sale. There should be a good flow of traffic and the site should be easy for shoppers to find. If not on a major thoroughfare, the sale location should be near something relatively identifiable by most people in your town.

2. **Parking** is often a problem. If shoppers cannot find convenient, safe parking they will definitely not stop and shop at your sale. Designate one parking spot closest to your sale as a "loading zone" and reserve it for those carrying merchandise to their cars.

3. The specific **building** used for your sale should be suitable in terms of both the amount and type of space available. If the building is a decrepit old warehouse, shoppers are less likely to stop and shop than if your sale is held in a neat looking garage or commercial building. If the building is too large, your merchandise may look very inadequate.

Home--Yours, Neighbors, Friends, etc.

The vast majority of garage sales are held at someone's home. If you decide to hold yours at home, consider the following questions:

1. Do you really want to hold the sale at your home?

2. Is it necessary to obtain a permit to do so?

3. Do you have sufficient space to effectively display your merchandise?

4. Is there sufficient parking?

5. Can potential buyers find your sale easily?

6. What about neighbors--are they likely to get upset with extra traffic and noise from your sale or would they be willing to participate in a neighborhood sale?

> *"If a man write a better book,*
> *preach a better sermon,*
> *or make a better mousetrap*
> *than his neighbor,*
> *tho he build his house*
> *in the woods,*
> *the world will make a beaten*
> *path to his door"*
> *.....R. W. Emerson, 1803-1882*

Garage

Holding a sale in the garage provides you with a relatively easily cleared space of about 300 square feet in a single car garage, 550 square feet in a double car garage. Finding that much clear space in any other part of a home is usually difficult, if not impossible. Garage doors are large enough to move bulky items in and out with ease. The driveway and areas around the garage may also be used as display space.

Since garages are used to store many things besides cars, most take some cleaning and preparation before they are suitable locations for a sale. In addition to removing or covering non-sale items, adding extra lighting and backgrounds takes more than a casual effort. Fortunately, most of us can leave the car(s) outside for a few days while the sale is being set up and taken down.

Of course, the one of the advantages to holding your sale in the garage is the ability to truly label yours a "Garage Sale!"

Basement

Basements are not good locations for a sale unless yours happens to have a direct access at ground level. Most often basement stairways are narrow and available space is tight. Often the basement provides direct access to the rest of the house, so security can be a problem. While not all basements are dark and dingy, most people have that impression and tend to shy away from basement sales.

Yard

Your yard can be used as an excellent sale location provided you don't mind folks walking all over your landscaping. Containing the sale area can be difficult unless your yard is fenced. While there may be a great amount of display space, the most obvious disadvantage is total dependence on the weather. Unless you plan to erect tents or shelters, planning a yard sale can be very risky indeed.

Porch, Patio

A covered porch or patio can be used as a sale location by itself or in addition to some other sale area. Either will work well since the area is well defined and access is limited. There may be direct access to the rest of your house, so plan to keep that under control. In all but the worst kind of weather, a covered porch or patio should provide adequate shelter for both your merchandise and your shoppers.

House Itself

There are times when a sale can be held in the house itself. If your inventory consists almost entirely of furniture or appliances that could be most effectively displayed in place then use of your house as a display area may be warranted. Many estate sales use the house as a primary sale location, simply tagging each item where it stands. Sales that do not have a lot of merchandise to sell often use the house as a sale location to prevent shoppers from simply driving by and examining the inventory.

Using your house as a sale location is, however, fraught with potential problems:

1. Traffic flow through most houses is not conducive to large crowds of people.

2. Unless you plan to use plastic runners or throw rugs, a parade of shoppers through your house leaves a mess.

3. Limiting the sale area to a room or two may be the only way to block access to other areas of the house.

4. Potential burglars may be very interested in what else is in the house for a later visit.

5. Moving large furniture pieces or appliances out of most houses is difficult.

Many shoppers are reluctant to browse at sales conducted in houses because the anonymity of the garage sale is lost when you go inside a house. It is much easier to walk in and out of a garage without feeling any obligation.

Apartment

Apartment sales face the same advantages and disadvantages as sales in the house. There are some additional advantages, however:

1. Apartment complexes are usually easier to find than individual homes.

2. The proximity of neighbors increases the chances of organizing multiple unit sales at the same time.

Here are some potential disadvantages to apartment sales:

1. Locating an individual apartment in a complex can be a problem unless some very well made signs are used to direct traffic.

2. Advertising needs to convince potential shoppers there is enough merchandise to make your sale a worthwhile stop.

3. Access for moving large pieces of merchandise is often more limited than in an individual home, particularly if the apartment is not at ground level.

4. Most apartment complexes have limited parking facilities, so some cooperation from your neighbors will be required in order to provide short term parking for your customers. Signs indicating where to park for the sale will be very helpful.

5. Many apartment complexes have a restriction in their rental agreement regarding sales. Be sure to consult the management in your complex prior to planning a sale, since the penalties imposed for non compliance with rental agreements are often rather stiff.

If there are garages available at your complex, perhaps you could arrange to rent one for a short time and hold your sale there or arrange with one of your friends to hold your sale in his garage.

Commercial Facilities

Often commercial facilities can be rented for a short term sale for a surprisingly low fee. The most obvious candidates for short term rental are vacant store buildings. Most store buildings will have the advantage of being in a high traffic location and provide a relatively large clear space in which to set up merchandise displays. If you don't have a lot to sell, however, it will look like even less if you put it in a large building. The best use of a fairly large commercial building would be for a multi-family or group sale featuring a broad selection of merchandise.

Portions of parking lots can often be rented when the business that owns the lot is closed. In most cases, this means that rentals are confined to weekends--but that is also the best time for garage sales! If the parking lot is paved, you will save a lot of potential mess if the weather turns nasty. Using a temporary shelter (such as a tent or canopy) will provide protection from the weather. Since this will be a high visibility sale with no provision for closing for the night, parking lot sales are most often single day affairs.

Tents

An increasing number of sales are being held in tents! Large tents are available for rent in most areas and create enough curiosity from passers-by to virtually guarantee a crowd at your sale. It is wise to choose a high traffic location to erect the tent, perhaps even a parking lot as we discussed in the last section.   Since rental costs are relatively high, you may want several families involved in this type of sale.   Display space available depends on the size of the tent, but will be larger than many garages.   It is easy to create a festive atmosphere for a tent sale through creative use of signs, entertainment, refreshments and decorations.   Be sure to consider the need for electricity, rest rooms for the workers and containing traffic flow for security purposes.

Mini-Storage Warehouses

Mini-Storage warehouses, if they are available in your area, make excellent locations for garage sales.   Some will rent garage size stalls for a short period of time and often you can rent more than one if you need additional space.   Usually these warehouses are relatively easy for shoppers to find and have enough parking for most sales.   Security problems associated with holding a sale at your own home are virtually eliminated.

You will need to be sure that electricity is available and the lighting is at least adequate. You will probably have to pay a cleaning deposit, but if you clean up after your sale that is usually refundable.   Check on liability insurance in case one of your shoppers should happen to have an accident--arrange for short term coverage if necessary.

Flea Markets And Group Sales

Many churches, charitable groups and private organizations sponsor flea markets or specialty sales at which you can rent space for a small fee. This arrangement has several advantages:

1. It gives you a good sale location that is away from your own home.

2. The organizers will have taken care of publicity.

3. There is something of a shopping mall effect in that customers tend to buy more when a better variety of merchandise is displayed.

Along with the advantages, there are some distinct disadvantages to flea markets and group sales:

1. Display space may be limited either by availability or cost.

2. All the merchandise to be sold must be transported to the sale location, often precluding selling large appliances or furniture.

3. Shoppers will carefully compare prices without necessarily looking closely at the quality of merchandise offered, meaning you may have to accept less for some of your items than you would at an individual sale.

A Few Last Thoughts On Location.

If you can't find (or afford) an ideal location for your sale, don't worry. Creative promotion and advertising can definitely help to minimize the drawbacks of a marginal location.

The range of items offered at garage sales is almost mind boggling. Some items you think will never sell are among the first to go. On the other hand, you may end up almost giving away some things you feel are genuine bargains. **The safest rule of thumb is NEVER assume you know what will sell and what won't.** There is an old saying that states "You'll never go broke underestimating the taste of the American People." Nowhere is that more true than in the area of garage sales.

SELECTING MERCHANDISE

In this section, we'll discuss specifics of selecting the merchandise for your sale. Although we'll cover a lot of items, you will probably be able to come up with many more. Trust your own judgment and, if in doubt, include it in your sale. The worst that can happen is that the item won't sell and who knows--it just might!

Your Own

The most obvious place to begin looking for garage sale merchandise is right in your own home. Look over everything you own with a critical eye as to whether or not you would want to sell it. Be sure to look everywhere! Start with the attic and work downward or the basement and work up. Look in every box, drawer, closet and cabinet. Put everything to be included in the sale in one place. Don't worry about organization right now--just stack everything together.

Recruit as much help as you need to conduct your search. Get the whole family involved and agree in advance how the proceeds from items they locate will be divided. Establishing a purpose for the sale, such as financing a family vacation, may result in much more enthusiastic cooperation from everyone.

Once you've finished the house, search your garage from top to bottom. The rafters of our garage hold a veritable treasure of good garage sale merchandise. Don't forget the trunk of the car and any other places you've stashed anything!

Most people are surprised by the number of items they find in their own home. If you are diligent in your search, you should be well on your way to having plenty of merchandise for a good garage sale.

Others

Once the word gets out that you are planning a garage sale, other people will want to be involved. Friends, relatives and neighbors always have "just a couple of things" to contribute. If you encourage them, they may find a lot more items. Set ground rules for the quality of merchandise before agreeing to accept any for your sale. Don't let your sale become a garbage dump! If they are convinced you are serious about making a lot of money from your sale, most folks will leave the garbage at home and bring items that will let them in on some of this financial action.

Special Buys From Other Sales

If you follow the suggestions in this book, you will have shopped a number of other sales prior to setting up your own. By getting a good idea of prices and demand in your area, you will certainly be able to identify significant bargains when you see them. Buy merchandise to resell if you feel there is a reasonable chance of making a profit on it. Be selective and buy only those items you are quite sure will sell rapidly.

One effective tactic is to buy specific kinds of merchandise from other sales and run a specialty sale of your own. Most sales, for instance, feature only a smattering of children's toys, baby goods, books, tools, sporting goods, etc. Decide on a specialty area and build up a supply of merchandise by shopping a lot of sales. If each item you purchase is priced low enough, you should be able to resell it at a profit.

Auctions

Many people who attend auctions regularly get some fantastic bargains. If you know your merchandise and prices, auctions offer a fun way of accumulating merchandise for your garage sale.

The secret to getting good merchandise at auctions is to set a mental price on each item before the bidding starts. If you are able to buy the item at or below your target price, chances are you will have gotten a bargain. It takes a great deal of self control not to exceed your price limit when bidding gets spirited. Just remember you are buying for resale.

New

If you shop the clearance racks at your favorite store, you will occasionally run across merchandise at prices so low that it is possible to resell at a profit. In order to do this successfully, you will need to consider the demand and potential selling price of each item. If you feel it will sell at your garage sale, give it a try!

Craft items are often sold at garage sales. If you offer some reasonably priced craft items, chances are they will sell. **Garage sales are not the place to sell high priced craft items, however.** They will do much better at a craft sale or consignment shop.

Baked goods and refreshments can also add significantly to the profitability of your sale. Check local regulations before offering either.

To Sell More, Show More

Retailers understand the importance of selection and go to great lengths to insure that their customers have plenty of merchandise from which to choose. If your sale has very little merchandise to offer, potential shoppers will not spend much time looking at what's there. Just getting shoppers to leave their cars is difficult if they feel the effort is not worthwhile. Do whatever is necessary to have plenty of merchandise on hand.

LARGE HOUSEHOLD GOODS

There is some demand for large household goods at garage sales. Although most customers are looking for small, easily transported items, there are always shoppers looking for bargain priced furniture or appliances.

Furniture

Moving sales have traditionally been the prime source of furniture items, but we have seen furniture at many garage sales. Overstuffed furniture is almost always hard to sell, although we have sold some to landlords who rent furnished apartments and newlyweds who couldn't afford new.

Wooden furniture items are always popular, particularly if they are in good condition. Dining sets, bookcases, entertainment centers, chairs and curio cabinets will fetch good prices. Bedroom sets are particularly high demand items, although old mattresses should not be included in your sale.

Other furniture items, particularly those in poor condition may not sell. Furniture that can be easily reupholstered or refinished sells much easier than chrome and plastic pieces that have seen better days.

Appliances

If you have appliances for sale, demonstrate that they work or be able to tell potential buyers what repairs are needed. Refrigerators and freezers are much better sellers than ranges or dishwashers. Air conditioners, space heaters, humidifiers, dehumidifiers and other seasonal appliances sell best in the early part of their season. It's no problem to sell an air conditioner or fan on a 100 degree day, but you may have some difficulty selling it when frost is in the air.

Bedding

As mentioned earlier in this section, old mattresses should be discarded when you no longer need them. Baby and water bed mattresses are an exception since they are usually vinyl covered and easily disinfected. Box springs can be sold, as can sleeper couches, rather easily.

Linen bedding items, as long as they are clean and in good repair, are popular sale items. Quilts, handmade blankets, embroidered sheets and pillow cases, afghans and unusual bedspreads are high demand items and will fetch premium prices. **Be particularly careful when selling quilts--the actual value may surprise you!**

SMALL HOUSEHOLD GOODS

Small household items are the backbone of most garage sales. It is easy to see what was popular last Christmas by looking at a few sales. Many good items that have been used rarely, if ever, are hot sellers at garage sales. Recently, we've seen thousands of popcorn poppers, hot dog cookers, automatic coffee makers, hot curlers and hair dryers. If you look carefully around your house, you'll probably find many appliances and gadgets that have rarely, if ever, been used. Garage sale shoppers are tempted to buy these gadgets for the same reasons you did--but at a fraction of the price you paid!

Recently, we combined two households and moved--a marvelous opportunity to look through everything and decide what was and what wasn't worth moving. Even we were surprised by what we found. After a gigantic garage sale, we had considerably fewer hair dryers, electric frying pans, popcorn poppers, waffle irons, casserole dishes, curling irons, mixers, pots and pans, canister sets, "Tupperware", can openers, etc., etc.

If you have more than a few back shelf items at your house, consider selling them. To put it colloquially, **"If it has more than an inch of dust on it, SELL IT!"**

SPORTING GOODS

All types of sporting goods are popular garage sale items. Used rackets, bats, balls, helmets, fishing equipment, skates and golf clubs will almost always sell if the price is right. If you look carefully around the house, you will probably find some baseball gloves, basketball hoops, footballs, skis or other pieces of sporting equipment that you or your children have outgrown or just no longer use. One of the most popular items at our last several sales has been used golf balls. Most of them were too beat up to be used in regular play, but sold rapidly when offered for practice at a quarter each.

Firearms

It is possible to sell firearms at a garage sale, but not necessarily a good idea to do so. You must check local, state and federal regulations very closely before offering any shotguns, rifles or handguns for sale. In most states the sale of handguns is strictly regulated and the buyer must possess a permit to own the weapon BEFORE buying it. Rifles and shotguns are not quite so rigorously controlled, but regulations vary from state to state.

There could also be some unexpected legal complications if the buyer of your firearms uses them in an illegal manner. You could be held responsible for things entirely beyond your control!

Any firearms you do offer for sale should be UNLOADED, thoroughly cleaned, oiled and kept well out of the reach of children. Do not keep ammunition close at hand, for obvious reasons.

Group Sets

Volleyball, badminton, croquet and other group activity sets are in demand and usually bring a good price. The set should be complete as possible and attractively packaged to bring top dollar.

Big Ticket Items

Very expensive items such as motorcycles, boats, outboard motors, ATV's or snowmobiles will not bring near what they are worth and probably would be better sold through a classified newspaper ad than at a garage sale. Just having your big ticket item displayed, however, may stimulate someone to tell a friend about what you have for sale. Have a printed sheet describing the item, your name and phone number and any other pertinent information available to hand out.

TOOLS

Tools of all kinds are high demand items at garage sales. If you have any quantity of them to sell, be sure to mention that fact specifically in your advertising. Most popular are small power tools (drills, saws, sanders, routers) but larger tools such as table saws, drill presses or air compressors will usually sell if the price is reasonable.

If you have only one or two large tool items to sell, it would be better to try to sell them with a classified newspaper ad. By running the ad a few weeks prior to your garage sale, you can always offer the items in your sale if classified advertising does not produce a buyer. This is particularly true when the items will appeal only to a very limited group of people. A woodworking lathe or elaborate welder, for example, would probably not generate much interest at a garage sale.

Lawn and garden tools are particularly good sellers, especially if you offer them at the early part of their season for use. Lawn mowers, nylon line trimmers, edgers, spreaders sell well at spring sales; snow blowers and shovels in the fall. Rototillers and other power tools do well almost any time of the year. Be sure to mention the larger items in your advertising. Describe them in detail if you feel that will help create shopper interest and merit the extra expense.

Hand tools of all types and small power tools will bring excellent prices as long as they are in relatively good condition. Some tools, such as the Craftsman line from Sears, are guaranteed for life and will be replaced if they break. Making your shoppers aware of that fact will enable you to charge significantly more for those tools. Be sure your tools are clean, sharp and operational to bring top dollar for them.

CLOTHES

Clothing is an extremely variable item--some garage sales sell a great deal of clothing, others do not. As we will discuss in a later chapter, the way in which clothing is displayed is critical in determining whether or not it will sell.

Adult clothing is quite season dependent. It has been our experience that items that can be used as disposable work clothes will often sell much faster than more fashionable items in better condition. Any specialty items (such as maternity clothes, uniforms, tuxedos, cocktail dresses, etc.) should be clearly identified and displayed separately.

Children outgrow more clothes than they wear out, so almost everyone who has children ends up with a surplus of perfectly good clothing that can be used by other families. Many garage sale shoppers look for children's clothes and appreciate the opportunity to buy them at a fraction of the new cost. The nice thing about children's clothing styles is that they don't really change much from year to year. Ninja Turtles replaced Strawberry Shortcake who replaced Care Bears, but those are more for the parent's benefit than children's preferences. As long as children's clothes are clean and in good repair, they'll usually sell. Some items will bring considerably more money if sold just before or in the early part of their prime use season (snowsuits in the fall, sundresses and shorts in the spring, etc.).

All clothing must be well organized and displayed. Most shoppers will not dig through a large heap of items on a table, but will "ooh" and "aah" at pretty clothes attractively displayed. A few minutes spent darning and washing will pay big dividends in the selling price of your clothing items. In order to sell well, clothing must be clean and in good repair--although tattered jeans seem to be the exception to this rule. We sold several pairs with ease at our last sale.

Old, worn out clothes can be packaged as rags and sold that way. Quilters and rag carpet makers like to buy packages of colorful rags for use in their crafts. Others will buy them just for cleaning around the house.

BABY ITEMS

Baby goods almost always sell at garage sales, but only if they are clean and in good condition. Cribs, playpens, highchairs, swings, car seats, scales, nursery monitors and changing tables are in demand and will usually command a premium price.

Toys for babies should be displayed right along with all the other baby items in your sale. Be sure the toys are intact and have no loose pieces.

Wash your toys with a disinfecting solution prior to offering them for sale.

Infant blankets, sheets and bedding are good items to place in your sale as long as they are clean and in good repair. Handmade baby items such as booties, clothing, afghans, quilts and toys should not be overlooked when selecting merchandise to sell.

Baby items are one of the best categories of merchandise to accumulate at other sales and feature in a specialty sale of your own. Any sale advertising a large selection of baby goods is sure to be a hit!

TOYS

Toys, like clothes, are usually outgrown. Kids tend to lose interest in toys long before they are worn out. While toys that are badly damaged or completely destroyed should be discarded, serviceable toys can be sold at a garage sale. This is particularly true of more expensive and sturdy toys such as Fisher-Price or Little Tykes.

Before offering any toys in your garage sale, be sure to establish ownership. If they belong to your children, make some financial arrangement or get the children involved in the sale. There is nothing more disconcerting to a shopper than to have a child clinging tenaciously to some toy he has just purchased!

Toys should be complete as possible. Those with small parts should be in plastic bags or have the pieces taped together to prevent them from getting lost. Battery powered toys will sell much faster if they are equipped with batteries and can be demonstrated. Your toys will bring much better prices if they are clean and in good repair. A little paint, glue or other minor repair help your toys look like new again.

LINENS

Linens like sheets, blankets, pillowcases, bedspreads, tablecloths and towels are popular garage sale items and usually sell readily. Curtains, drapes and blinds (unless they are a very popular size) are more difficult to sell, although creative display can help considerably.

Like clothing, linens should be clean and in good repair. Particularly interesting pieces should be displayed separately to bring top dollar.

We have sold boxes and boxes of old beach towels at each of our sales, the good ones for use as towels and the battered ones for use as rags. If you have old, beat-up linens, put them in bags and sell them as rags--you'll be amazed at how fast they sell!

AUTOMOTIVE

We have never had much luck selling automobiles at any of our sales, although a few shoppers expressed interest in some of them. Perhaps the reason we didn't sell the last one was the engine that had just blown up on the highway! Or maybe it was the body riddled with rust spots.

Could it have been the passenger seat that reclined whenever someone tried to sit in it?

Items like ramps, oil drip pans, grease guns, buffers, car vacuum cleaners and add-ons for cars are of particular interest to many shoppers. Electronic items like CB radios, stereos, tape decks, radar detectors and portable telephones are quick to sell if they are priced correctly and at least reasonably current. You will have a great deal of difficulty giving away an AM-only radio or 8 track tape player, although you could pay shoppers to take them (no kidding--see chapter 5).

The best selling automotive items are those not limited to a specific make and model. Items that can be used with any car such as cleaning materials, polishes, wax, chamois cloths or replacement fluids will sell as long as they don't look damaged.

As mentioned earlier, tools are always big hits with weekend mechanics. Specialized automotive tools such as timing lights, heavy duty jacks, body shop sanders, or engine diagnostic kits should be mentioned specifically in your advertising.

JEWELRY

Almost everyone has a collection of jewelry they no longer wear, some of it in nearly new condition. While jewelry does not wear out in the same way that clothes do, tastes change and most of us replace inexpensive jewelry pieces more often than our wardrobes.

Costume Jewelry

The best selling jewelry at garage sales falls into two general categories--costume jewelry that is cheap but looks expensive and any other jewelry that is unique and relatively inexpensive. Unless you advertise specific pieces of jewelry, most of your sales will be limited to those items selling for just a few dollars each.

A garage sale is the perfect opportunity to get rid of some of your collection of costume jewelry and watches. There is a demand for wind-up watches of all types, particularly pocket watches. Some ornate pocket watches can fetch tidy prices from collectors, so be sure to check a pricing guide before offering one in your garage sale.

There really is no limit to the variety of jewelry items to be found at garage sales. You've heard the expression "One person's junk is another person's treasure." Costume jewelry provides us with many examples. The pin or necklace you bought to go with a particular piece of clothing may be just what some shopper is looking for. Since jewelry rarely wears out, it tends to remain long after the clothes are gone.

Garage sale shoppers impulse buy jewelry more than any other item. Some buy for gifts, but most buy just for themselves. Parents will purchase some very inexpensive jewelry items for their kids to play "dress up". Teens are a good market for jewelry items and, with their ever changing tastes, are likely to buy most anything.

Jewelry accessories like cleaners, organizers and storage boxes are popular garage sale items. Musical jewelry boxes, in particular, have become quite a collectors item and may bring a much better price than you would expect.

Valuable Items

In the interests of safety (discussed at some length in Chapter 9), it is best not to offer expensive pieces of jewelry at a garage sale. Eliminate the temptation for shoplifting and theft by not displaying costly items. If you have just a couple of expensive jewelry pieces and want to try to sell them, be sure to follow the guidelines outlined in Chapter 9.

COSMETICS

Many cosmetic sales people sell brand new, items at their garage sales. We've seen a lot of Avon, Fuller and Mary Kay merchandise in particular. Often these are samples or discontinued items that have never been opened. Sellers recover some of their investment and buyers can pick up some real bargains. Most salespeople also offer a selection of current items at a slight discount off the usual price. This is a good way for the customer to save money and the salesperson to gain new clients.

The key to selling any quantity of cosmetics is effective display. Some people offer cosmetics stacked in large boxes and expect shoppers to rummage through to find what they want. Others creatively display their cosmetics using attractive fixtures, good lighting and colorful backgrounds.

The difference in shopper interest between the two approaches is dramatic. Cosmetics well displayed not only sell much faster, but at considerably better prices than those stacked in boxes.

If you have cosmetics to sell, mention them in your advertising. Be descriptive enough so potential shoppers will know exactly what you have to offer. Rather than just stating "Cosmetics", try something like "Large quantity of new, sample and discontinued AVON products at bargain prices". Since catalogs are definitely part of your on-going advertising efforts, have plenty of them available for shoppers who might be interested becoming regular customers.

PHOTOGRAPHIC

Video cassette recorders (VCR's), video cameras with or without built in recorders and video accessories are high demand items. Many of the first and second generation units are being replaced with newer, smaller, more capable and higher quality pieces. Your old equipment may be just what a shopper is looking for. As long as it works and the price is reasonable, you should have no trouble selling video equipment at your garage sale.

Still cameras come in all shapes and sizes. A few years ago disk cameras were the rage, now compact 35mm units have captured the market. Instant cameras are not as popular as they once were, but are still in demand. Dust off your cameras, put in fresh batteries if needed, check to be sure they work and film is still available (You may want to include a roll in the sale price). Do not leave film in regular or movie cameras. Taking a picture of a shopper with an instant camera, however, may quickly clinch a sale.

The market for movie cameras and projection equipment has really dried up with the advent of inexpensive video equipment. If you have movie equipment to sell, be sure to price it VERY reasonably and cross your fingers! Slide projectors and screens may sell if they are recent and include some extra slide trays.

Old cameras and some of their accessories have become collectors items and can bring good prices in the right circles. Unfortunately, garage sales are not the right circles. Consult one of the pricing guides listed in the Appendices or a dealer if you have old camera equipment that you think may be valuable.

Darkroom equipment, electronic flashes, tripods, carrying cases and other photographic accessories sell well at most garage sales. If you show a sample picture or demonstrate how an accessory works, the asking price can be significantly higher. Be sure to put fresh batteries in those items that need them.

ELECTRONICS

Electronics is a wide open category of merchandise that includes any number of items. As mentioned earlier, VCR's and Camcorders are high demand items. Ditto for stereo components such as receivers, tape decks, CD players, speakers and equalizers. Television sets are extremely popular at garage sales. All these are relatively big ticket items that most shoppers will want assurances work OK. If possible, set up your display area so these items can be easily demonstrated or, if you prefer, operate them during the sale. Some items require other pieces of equipment to demonstrate--for example, a VCR needs a television set. If you use a TV set for just that purpose, be sure to mark it plainly "Not For Sale". Non-working items should be clearly labeled as such and priced accordingly.

Relatively recent computers may not attract a lot of interest at a garage sale since the prices for brand new units have dropped so dramatically in the last couple of years. Video games, on the other hand, are hot sellers. Small electronic items such as keyboards, clock radios, digital clocks, personal stereos of the "Walkman" variety can be best sold by demonstrating to shoppers that they work and are worth the asking price.

Calculators, particularly the printing variety, are in great demand. Putting a fresh battery, roll of paper and ribbon (if needed) in your calculator will up the potential selling price significantly.

In contrast to the potentially good selling items we have listed in this section, console stereos (the old wooden "coffin" types), single function video games, 8 track tape players, broken television sets and desperately outmoded computers are likely to find a permanent home in your garage. These may be good candidates for the "We'll pay you to take these" display that discussed in chapter 5.

Baked Goods, Refreshments

There have been many combination garage-bake sales in our area, often sponsored by civic or church groups. We attended one sale this past summer sponsored by a group of cub scouts. One of the young boys asked us if we would like to purchase a bag of cookies he quite honestly described as "burned"--we did. He was just too cute to turn down. I wonder how many bags of cookies he sold before whoever baked them found out why they were so popular!

Baked goods will sell if they are attractive and priced reasonably. Take a hint from supermarkets and have minuscule samples of some of the more popular items available. Shoppers are often unimpressed by displays of items, but cannot resist some tasty item they have just had the opportunity to sample. Be sure your baked goods are packaged and displayed attractively. A trick frequently used in shopping malls is to have something baking during the sale--the aroma is guaranteed to increase the sale of your baked goods.

One of the real success stories in our area has been the "Unbaked Sale" which features homemade items ready to bake in your own oven. For this type of sale, you will want to have at least one of each item baked so shoppers can see, smell and taste it. The balance of your inventory can be refrigerated or, in the case of a multiple day sale, frozen. Be sure to include complete baking instructions in each package. So many working folks would love to have the time to bake homemade goodies. The "Unbaked Sale" gives them that opportunity and provides an excellent method of raising money for your group (or yourself).

Edible handmade items such as jams, jellies, pickles or preserves have been runaway best sellers at both craft and garage sales I've attended. Before offering edible items, however, check local regulations regarding such sales.

Refreshments such as coffee, lemonade or iced tea are often sold at garage sales. It makes more business sense to give them away. After all, it is difficult to drive off while drinking a cup of coffee. Anything that encourages shoppers to spend more time at your sale greatly enhances the prospects for its success. If you can't afford to give away refreshments, price them very reasonably. You should use disposable cups or glasses and provide a trash basket for their disposal. Napkins should be provided so any spills can be promptly remedied.

CRAFTS

While we will discuss craft sales in another chapter, there are many opportunities for featuring some craft items at garage sales. Interesting displays of craft items have sold very well at sales in our area.

It is important to separate the craft items from the rest of your merchandise and display them prominently. Signs may be posted to identify the nature of these items and their prices. Lower priced, less labor intensive craft items seem to sell best. Garage sale shoppers are rarely willing to pay for the amount of time and skill involved in an intricate needlework piece or elaborate woodcarving.

You may decide to accept some craft items on consignment for your garage sale, as long as they meet the criteria we just outlined.

PLANTS

There have been some interesting displays of plants at recent sales in our area. The plants were reasonably priced and sold very well. If you are blessed with a green thumb, it might prove very profitable to offer some plants at your next garage sale.

It does take some advance planning to start plants at the right time. New plants should be the right size for transplanting just before your sale. It is not necessary to put your plants in fancy containers--peat or inexpensive clay pots work very well. You can, of course, use more elaborate planters and adjust the price to reflect the value of both the plant and container.

Artificial plants and flowers rarely generate the interest that live ones do. Effective displays and creative arrangements will definitely help sell any plant--live or artificial.

MISCELLANEOUS MERCHANDISE

As the heading suggests, this category can include almost anything. Recent sales in our area have featured such miscellaneous items as "Cool Whip" containers, old family pictures, sunlamps, hairbrushes (complete with a few stray hairs), used toilets, stuffed Moose, picnic baskets, knitting needles, light bulbs, packaged foods, sets of china, Christmas decorations, antique butter churns, canning jars, ash trays, wigs, sunglasses, etc., etc.

Garage sales always have miscellaneous items. One of the most interesting things about garage sale shopping is looking at the kinds of things people try to(and often do) sell. If you are on the selling side, it is fascinating to watch who buys which of your miscellaneous items. Some of the most off-the-wall items are among the first to sell.

You will have a group of items that can best be described as miscellaneous. As long as these items can be of some use to someone else, they are good candidates for your sale. Set what you think is a fair price and hope somebody will be interested. Most often garage sale shoppers will haggle if the price seems too high.

Remember, "It's not junk if someone will buy it!"

4

ANTIQUES AND COLLECTIBLES

Of all the items offered at garage sales, antiques and collectibles are the greatest source of potential profits for the seller. Initial cost, particularly for collectibles, has little relationship to the potential selling price. Although garage sale shoppers are not willing to pay dealer prices for antiques or collectibles, items in either class will bring far more than most other general merchandise items.

ANTIQUES

Some antique items, such as furniture, weather the years well and become very desirable additions to many homes. Even those who are not antique collectors may purchase an attractive piece or two for themselves. Antiques are frequently sold at garage sales--but the prices received are not as good as could be obtained elsewhere.

The most commonly collected antiques are furniture pieces. Garage sale shoppers are often interested in furniture that needs to be refinished or repaired, primarily because it is more affordable than items that are in prime condition. Dealers also prefer antiques in their original condition, adding the price of refurbishing to their resale prices. There are more reproductions than genuine antiques, so some sophistication is needed to identify genuine items. Garage sale

> *"Who will change old lamps for*
> *new ones?*
> *...new lamps for old ones?"*
> *.....Arabian Nights.*

shoppers will frequently buy antique **style** furniture simply because it strikes their fancy, whether or not it is authentic. Dealers, however, will make every effort to verify authenticity before purchasing anything.

Antique tools and domestic gadgets are a close second to furniture in popularity. Men tend to collect tools, while their wives look for household and kitchen gadgets. If you plan to offer items in either category, be prepared to explain the function of each item you have for sale. In the case of furniture, you should be able to tell what type of wood it contains. All antique items should be familiar enough so you can at least identify their function and approximate age. Pricing guides listed in the appendices may help you determine fair prices to ask for your antiques.

Books and art work tend to be good sellers. Antique clothing, unless it is in excellent condition and exceptionally interesting, may not sell. Durable antique items are, by far, the most popular items. China, glassware, candle holders, silverware and other durable pieces bring premium prices. Just removing the tarnish from a silver bowl or stains from china can double or triple the price shoppers are willing to pay. Do not, however, attempt to repair minor damage. Poorly done repairs will hurt an item's value more than a minor defect.

It is important that you be realistic about the antiques in your sale. Just because something is old does not necessarily make it valuable. Look carefully at the condition--chairs with broken legs and furniture with badly damaged parts will certainly not be as valuable as those in good condition. There are always shoppers looking for pieces to refurbish or specific parts for pieces they may already have, but they will buy them only if the price is very reasonable.

Display

Antiques can be displayed with all your other sale merchandise. It is important, however, that you identify the antique items with special labels or signs so shoppers will know they are special. If your antique is a large item, giving it plenty of space and light will make it stand out from the rest of your merchandise. You will find a few more ideas for displaying antiques in Chapter 7.

You can also create a separate display area for valuable antiques and restrict shopper traffic to that area. Enclose your antiques with some type of barrier, such as a rope or decorative chain. Be sure that shoppers can see all the items without having to touch them.

Another way of trying to sell antiques is to post a picture or description in the sale area with an invitation for shoppers to "ask to see" or "shown to interested buyers only." The assumption is, of course, that those interested in buying will flash a large bankroll and pursue the seller. Although this approach may have some advantages, potential buyers rarely do much pursuing.

COLLECTIBLES

Collectibles are those things that people accumulate for a specific reason. Some collectibles are widely advertised and easy to identify, such as commemorative plates and limited issue prints. Other things are collected by so many people that demand is high and they sell easily. Baseball cards, comic books, Hummel and Precious Moments figurines, Barbie dolls, beer cans and political memorabilia all fall into the latter category.

There are some categories of collectibles, however, that seem totally illogical to most of us. No matter the reason or the nature of their collection, collectors are interested in expanding their holdings and will do so at every opportunity.

Many people are convinced that collectibles are not only an interesting hobby, but an excellent way to make a substantial profit on a minimal investment. You will probably have at least some idea of the collectibility of most of the items in your sale. Check with price guides, dealers or local collectors if you are in doubt.

Collectors are typically sophisticated garage sale shoppers hunting for bargains and often find them. They know exactly the value of the items they are seeking, while sellers may be unaware of the collectibility of some of their merchandise.

Here is a list of some of the most frequently collected items:

Advertising Specialties
Badges
Baseball Cards
Cameras
Canes, Walking Sticks
Christmas Decorations
Coca Cola Items
Cracker Jack Toys
Cut Glass
Depression Glass
Dolls
Electric Trains
Fruit Jars
Golf Clubs
Handheld Fans
Comic Books
Kerosene Lamps
Military Items
Music Boxes
Neon Signs
Paperweights
Postcards & Stamps
Quilts
Railroad Memorabilia
Salt & Pepper Sets
Silver Service
Spoons
Stock Certificates
Telephone Insulators
Tools
World's Fair Items

Avon Bottles
Banks (coin)
Beer Cans & Bottles
Candleholders
Canning Jars
Clocks
Cookie Jars
Crystal
Decoys
Doilies, Lace
Doorknobs (Fancy)
Figurines
Glassware
Hand Tools
Hats, Hat Pins
Jewelry
Liquor Decanters
Movie Posters
Musical Instruments
Nutcrackers
Political Buttons
Prints
Radios
Records
Sheet Music
Snuff Boxes
Straight Razors
Teddy Bears
Thimbles
Watches, Watch Fobs

To all but the avid collector, prices you have set on collectibles may seem unreasonably high. You must decide how badly you want to sell each item--price it high and hope a serious collector comes along or price it low enough to appeal to even the most casual collector.

The pricing guides included in the Appendices will be of some help to you in determining what prices to ask for your collectibles. If you do not have enough to justify buying a price guide, check with your library--they may have a copy you can borrow.

Display

If you are offering collectibles in your garage sale, it is important that your display reflect the price you hope to get for them. Do not display valuable collectibles in the same way that you offer kitchen gadgets and miscellany.

Collectors like to buy items that have been well cared for. Often the packaging and condition of an item determine in large part the value of the item. Barbie Dolls in their original box, for example, are much more valuable than just the doll alone.

We will discuss display at some length in a later chapter, but let's establish here that proper display, cleanliness and good repair are vital factors in determining whether or not you will sell the collectibles in your inventory.

Advertising

In order to attract antique buffs and collectors to your garage sale, proper advertising is critical. Don't scrimp on the details. Rather than just listing "Hummel Christmas Plates," describe each in terms of the year of issue and condition. Be as specific as possible about the attributes of each of the valuable items you will be offering.

It is best not to include price information in your advertising. Buyers usually attempt to negotiate better prices anyway, so you are better off leaving prices out until the buyer has had an opportunity to examine each item.

Your advertising should be targeted to those dealers and collectors you hope to attract. In addition to advertising in the Garage Sale classification of your newspaper, be sure to include advertising in the Antique and Collectible categories. If there are clubs in your area, advertise your sale in their newsletter or have a friend announce it at a meeting.

Any collectors you know personally should receive a letter or flyer describing the items to be offered at your garage sale. Word of mouth is a strong advertising medium and should be exploited to the fullest. Offer a slight discount if the collector returns the flyer or brings a friend to your sale.

PLANNING YOUR SALE

A profitable garage sale requires a considerable amount of advance planning. As a matter of fact, one of the most common problems is letting the sale date sneak up without being adequately prepared. The time to plan is long before the sale, not as the first shoppers are coming up your driveway!

Check Laws

Many communities have ordinances regulating the frequency and duration of garage sales. It is rare to find any community that bans garage sales altogether, but most have limitations designed to prevent full time sales in residential areas. Some cities require that you obtain a permit to hold a sale, usually little more than a formality but important because your sale could be shut down for lack of the proper permit.

Virtually every community regulates the type and placement of signs, although these regulations are often overlooked for the occasional garage sale. One of the most frequent abuses is tacking signs to utility poles and not removing them punctually when a sale is finished. Nails used to attach signs are a hazard to utility workers who must climb those poles!

There are local, state and federal regulations about some of the items that could be sold at garage sales. Some of these items include

> *"The best laid schemes*
> *o'mice an' men*
> *Gang aft a-gley"*
> *.....Robert Burns, 1759-1796*

automobiles, motorcycles, firearms, animals, plants, and food. If you have any questions about specific items, check with local authorities.

Some states and local governments require garage sale holders to obtain a permit and collect sales tax. Often this requirement is waived for a short term sale, since the intent is to regulate sales operating as a business. Check with the local or state department of revenue for details.

Visit Other Sales

The best way to prepare for your own garage sale is to attend similar sales. This will help give you the customer's perspective and demonstrate the effectiveness of various methods of conducting a sale. Don't just look at the merchandise, look at how each sale is organized and conducted:

1. Check out displays to see which are most effective.

2. What kind of layout looks best to you?

3. What kinds of things attracted you to each sale?

4. How could some of the weak areas have been improved?

When looking at merchandise:

1. Get a feel for both the asking and selling prices of various items.

2. What kind of merchandise seems to be selling best?

3. What kinds of items are not selling?

4. Were shoppers asking for some items not displayed?

You will come across some outstanding bargains while attending these sales. Why not buy them to resell at your own sale? You will be spending some time and asking a lot of questions at each sale. Sale holders are much more willing to talk to paying customers!

Look carefully at advertising:

1. Compare the sale to the way it was described in the newspaper ads.

2. What kinds of signs are used and how effective are they?

3. Ask where advertising was done.

4. Compare the advertising cost to the number of customers you observe at each sale--is there a direct relationship?

5. Ask a few customers how they heard about the sales.

As noted in the beginning of this section, the primary reason to attend other sales is to gather ideas. You will find as many good ideas as bad ones. If a sale seems to be a resounding success, ask yourself what is making it that way? If it's a failure, see if you can figure out what's wrong. You can benefit from others experience and improve your own garage sale.

GENERAL SET-UP

Plan ahead and have some idea of how you would like your sale to look. This can range from Early Junk to Garage Sale Chic. You certainly don't want your sale to look like you dumped heaps of garbage on a table, but there is some risk in making your sale look too slick and professional. Shoppers can get the idea that attractive displays and good organization mean exorbitant prices. Leave some amateur touches to combat that mistaken notion.

The impression potential shoppers get when first seeing your sale is important--it determines whether or not they will stop and shop. **Anything you can do to create a good first impression will pay off handsomely.** Try balloons, banners, music, refreshments or whatever else you can think of. You don't necessarily need strolling musicians or circus clowns to sell your merchandise, but some means of interesting potential buyers is essential.

> *"It has long been an axiom of mine that the little things are infinitely the most important."*
> *...Sir Arthur Conan Doyle,*
> *1859-1930*

Space

Once you have selected and assembled your merchandise, you will have a pretty good idea how much display space will be needed. Be sure to plan for multi-level displays and use every inch to best advantage. One of the things we will be discussing later is how to construct displays that help you take advantage of every single inch of space.

We are often faced with a limited amount of space for a garage sale. If possible, it is very important to have enough space to effectively display all your merchandise. Cramming too much merchandise into too little space creates confusion and makes your sale look like a junk pile. It is not necessary to display all your merchandise at the same time. If you have several similar items, why not display them one at a time? As one sells, replace it with another.

Separate your space into sale and non-sale areas. It is confusing for shoppers to see a lot of "not for sale" items in the area and time consuming to answer questions as to what is and what is not for sale. You can use backgrounds to effectively separate areas. If your space is indoors, backgrounds can be hung from clotheslines circling the perimeter of your display area. Sheets, blankets, tarps or tablecloths may be used as backgrounds and also as additional display space.

Create more sale space outdoors with canopies and tents. Although you can define sales areas with fences and borders, it is foolhardy to depend on the weather. You can rent a canopy for a very reasonable price if you don't have access to one. In addition to keeping off the rain, a canopy or tent will keep shoppers protected from the sun. As a matter of fact, some neighborhoods pool their funds to sponsor a Neighborhood Tent Sale--a perfectly marvelous way to sell merchandise and keep peace in the neighborhood at the same time!

You can use space leading to your sale (sidewalks, driveway, etc.) for additional displays. Use this area for items that are not particularly weather sensitive and leave plenty of room for shoppers to carry goods away from the immediate sale area. You do not, however, want them stealing the merchandise, so keep a close eye on anything displayed in a direct traffic path.

Cleanliness

It is VERY important that both your sale area and merchandise be as clean as you can make them. This is important for two reasons:

1. You must attract shoppers to your sale. Most people will not even bother to stop at a sale that looks filthy.

2. The prices you get for your merchandise will be markedly better IF each item is as clean and attractive as possible.

Spend some time cleaning the sale area prior to setting up. It's much easier to clean when you don't have to dodge a lot of displays. Pay particular attention to grease on the floor if you're using a garage and cobwebs wherever you will be.

If there is grease or oil on the floor, clean it with a grease absorber. Ground in grease can sometimes be removed from cement floors using a heavy application of a spray oven cleaner, degreaser available at auto supply stores or salt sprinkled directly on the grease.

Each piece of merchandise must be cleaned and presented in the best possible way. Garage sale shoppers will buy items that are not cleaned and polished, but only at give-away prices. Are you willing to settle for a small fraction of the price you could get by showing all the potential of each item? The time spent cleaning and polishing your merchandise will pay off handsomely.

Lighting

One of the most common faults of garage sales is too little light. You cannot expect shoppers to be enthusiastic about stepping from bright sunlight outdoors into a "black hole of Calcutta" sale. It takes a while for the eyes to become accustomed to less light and shoppers may not be willing to stay around long enough to get a good look at your merchandise.

As a general rule, you will need enough light so the best points of every piece of merchandise can be easily seen. Take a lesson from retail stores-- few successful stores are dimly lit.

The first, and most obvious, source of light is sunlight from outdoors:

1. If your sale is in a garage or large building, the doors and windows will provide some internal

lighting. Be sure the windows are clean and remember they can also be used as display space for items requiring a great deal of light to be seen at their best.

2. Light colored backgrounds create an illusion of light and space. Backgrounds can consist of light colored fabrics (such as sheets or tablecloths), white Styrofoam panels, plywood or paneling covered with white shelf paper, or the light colored walls of a building.

3. Aluminum foil or white paper can be used to transform an otherwise dark surface into a light reflector. Reflectors strategically placed can help you take maximum advantage of light from doors and windows.

Here are some ways of providing artificial light in areas where sunlight doesn't reach:

1. Large areas can be lighted from above by fluorescent shop lights or incandescent reflectors. Either can be plugged into an extension cord and need not be permanently wired.

2. Extra light for special items can be provided by desk lamps, incandescent reflectors or lights strung around the immediate area.

3. Christmas light strings with white bulbs work very well for providing extra light and give you an extra bonus--**items displayed beneath bare bulbs always look more shiny** (that's

why you see bare bulbs strung around used car lots!)

4. Light all the lamps and light fixtures you have for sale. A clean, operating lamp will bring 2-3 times more money. You need not use large bulbs in sale lamps. Bulbs of 40-75 watts will provide plenty of light.

You will need heavy enough extension cords for artificial lights. If you are going to purchase a heavy cord, the best bet is one on a reel with several outlets and a circuit breaker of its own. Check with your hardware store for recommendations.

For sales that require a lot of artificial light, be sure to distribute the electrical load among several circuits. The typical 15-20 amp household circuit will operate about 1500 watts of lights. To estimate the requirements for your sale, just add up the wattage for each lamp you will be using. Don't forget to include some extra capacity for trying any electrically operated merchandise.

Traffic Flow

It is vital that you consider traffic flow when laying out your sale area. Plan for a logical entrance and exit area. Be sure there is a WELCOME sign or something special that will attract attention to the entrance. Balloons create a festive atmosphere and are inexpensive. Banners, flags, pinwheels or other attention getting devices may also be used. Set up your check out station at the exit and be sure it is clearly marked.

Do not make your layout so restrictive that shoppers cannot go back and pick up items they may have seen earlier. Arrange traffic flow so shoppers will pass all the display areas you have set up. Set up some little niches to demonstrate and allow customers to try things without tying up traffic for other shoppers.

If your layout is not straight in and out, shoppers will spend more time. Retailers know the amount of purchase is directly proportional to the amount of time shoppers spend in their store. **Try to get your shoppers to linger as long and look as much as possible.** If you are offering refreshments, station them near the exit so shoppers will feel obligated to spend a little more time and go back through some of your displays.

Perhaps you will decide to set up a "We'll Pay You To Take These" area (discussed elsewhere in this chapter). If so, position it in sight of the check out station and make it a fairly prominent display. Since the area will not be contributing directly to your total sales, it can be a little off the beaten path. A sign drawing attention to it's existence should be posted at both the entrance and check out areas. The mere existence of such an unusual display will probably create enough interest to keep shoppers around a little longer.

*'In baiting a mouse trap with cheese,
always leave room for the mouse'
.....H. H. Munro 1870-1916*

The best way to plan for traffic flow is to draw a sale layout on paper and indicate desired traffic flow with arrows. Draw the layout with chalk in the sale area, then walk around it to see if there are any problems. Before you set up any displays, walk around the layout again. Set up displays and try the traffic flow one last time before stocking your displays with merchandise.

Creature Comforts

If your sale is to be held indoors, providing for basic creature comforts is relatively easy. You need good ventilation if the weather is hot and heat if it is cold. It may be necessary to use supplementary fans or heaters to insure your shoppers are comfortable enough to linger a while. If the weather is rainy, mats or carpets to dry shoes will help avoid wet, slippery floors in the sale area.

Refreshments should be appropriate to the season. In warm weather, lemonade or ice water works well. Your kids might want to set up a beverage sale and charge a few pennies a glass-- this is a wonderful way to keep them occupied during the sale. In cooler weather coffee, hot chocolate or spiced cider will prove to be big hits.

A bench or several chairs can be set up to provide a resting area for those who might need it. Be sure this area is facing some displays and near any footwear that will require trying on.

Unless you are in a public building, it is usually not necessary (or desirable) to provide restroom or telephone facilities for your shoppers.

Check Out Area

The check out station should be near the exit and clearly identified by signs. While it is not necessary to have a computerized cash register at the check out area, you should provide at least some type of secure cash box, a calculator and bags for carrying merchandise.

Be sure someone is stationed at the check out during the time that your sale is in operation. From the check out area, you should be able to see all around the sale. Use a few mirrors if necessary.

Take a clue from supermarkets and display impulse purchase items near the check out station. Every extra item sold will contribute to the profitability of your sale! You should also put any relatively valuable items in plain sight of the check out station to help prevent shoplifting.

PRICING YOUR MERCHANDISE

This section will discuss one of the most critical parts of any sale--determining what prices to charge. If your prices are too low, you will sell a lot of merchandise but make too little money. On the other hand, if your prices are way too high you won't sell much. Ideally you should strike that delicate balance between asking too little or too much for each item. Pricing for garage sales tends to be an imprecise art that requires both the seller and buyer to be somewhat flexible.

General Considerations

Before we get to specific pricing guidelines, let's look at a few general considerations that must go in to determining prices.

Initial cost

The initial cost of an item is very often used as the primary yardstick of what to ask for it in a garage sale. In some cases, this may be a legitimate figure to use. If you purchased the item at a reasonable price and the price has not decreased drastically recently, then by all means use initial cost as your guideline for determining the asking price. If there is something unique about an item that justified a higher initial cost, point that out to potential buyers.

Are you in the habit of saving boxes or receipts for items you purchase? By leaving the price tag on the box, writing the initial price somewhere inconspicuous or keeping receipts for each item you purchase, you will have some sort of reference point. Of course you don't buy things just to sell them later in a garage sale, but the habit of writing prices and saving receipts will also prove useful in making an inventory of your possessions for insurance purposes.

Replacement cost

One of the buzzwords of the insurance industry is "replacement cost" which recognizes

> *"For what is worth in anything*
> *But so much money as 'twill bring"*
> *.....Samuel Butler, 1612-1680*

the fact that many items cost more to replace than they did to buy at some time in the past. The same principle applies to items you wish to sell. If you purchased an item several years ago and discover that similar items are selling for significantly more than you paid, by all means use the current price as your guideline in determining the asking price. The reverse is also true--if your item can be replaced for a fraction of what you paid, then you will have to consider replacement cost in determining what price to ask.

You can determine replacement cost for items by pricing them in local stores or finding similar items in catalogs such as those from Sears or Wards. If you don't have a catalog, they can be purchased for about $5.00 at either of the stores.

When looking at replacement cost, be sure to consider items with substantially the same features. An old Walkman stereo that just plays tapes will not bring anywhere near the price of a newer Walkman with AM-FM stereo tuner, automatic reverse, noise reduction, etc. Be realistic in comparing your item to newer ones with more features.

Age

Age can work for or against garage sale items. In some instances, older is equated with better. Old metal tools, for instance, are considered superior to contemporary plastic ones. Solid wood furniture is head and shoulders above the fiberboard and veneers used in some of today's offerings. If your items fall into this category, you can ask a premium price.

On the other hand, age is not kind to some types of merchandise. Plastic toys get brittle, electronics get outmoded, furniture gets worn and clothes fade. If your items are nearing (or have passed) the end of their useful life, you must adjust the asking price accordingly.

Condition

Often the condition of an item is directly related to its age. There are some types of items, however, more affected by the care they have received than their age. Glassware, artwork, silverware, jewelry, kitchen utensils, linens, guns and wood furniture are just a few examples of things that can be old and in surprisingly good condition. As in other areas, the reverse is also true--some items live a very hard life and are ready for the scrap heap long before their normal life span has passed. Look carefully at the condition of items you plan to sell before you set your prices.

Demand

Logic tells us that an item in demand will sell much better than one out of current favor. Nowhere is this more evident than in the teen market where fortunes are made overnight by offering a product that happens to catch the fancy of that age group. Tattered jeans, for example, have been hot items in the teen market over the last couple of years. The trick, of course, is to find just such a product and then create a demand by skillful advertising.

Most of us assume that shoppers will come with some built in demand for our merchandise.

This may be one of the most fundamental flaws and should be considered when pricing and advertising your merchandise. Something as simple as a sign explaining what an item does, an offer to show a potential buyer how it works or including an instruction book will significantly increase the demand (and selling price) for your merchandise.

Desire to dump

One of the primary reasons for having a garage sale is to get rid of unwanted items. Just how unwanted a particular item is will certainly weigh heavily into price considerations. The buyer will also be trying to gauge your "desire to dump" for price negotiations. **If you are anxious to get rid of an item, price it accordingly.**

You can use items that you are really anxious to get rid of as loss leaders in the same way that retail stores offer a few items at very low prices just to attract shoppers. The purpose is to get shoppers to look around and buy additional items at higher prices. Garage sales can use this tactic to good advantage by scattering a few loss leaders throughout the displays to peak shoppers interest.

There will be a few things that you absolutely, positively do not want to keep. While you could give them away, you will find a better solution

> *"Most human beings have an almost infinite capacity for taking things for granted."*
> *...Aldous Huxley, 1894-1963*

within the next few pages. If you can't wait, just read ahead to the section entitled "Never Give Away!" We'll wait for you to get back and then discuss rules of thumb for pricing merchandise.

RULES OF THUMB

While there are as many exceptions as applications for most rules, here are a few that may help you in setting prices:

Even dollar prices

Retailers use .95 or .99 at the end of their prices, assuming that most shoppers will not realize that 14.99 is just a penny short of $15.00. Such pricing tactics are resented by garage sale shoppers. Using odd cent amounts forces you to stockpile a great deal of change and increases the chances of errors while handling money.

While it is not really practical to set prices only at even dollars, you can use 25 cents as your lowest price. This is important for your lower priced items, since many of them won't be worth a dollar. If you have items worth less than a quarter, offer them in multiples of two or three for a quarter. Once you get over $5.00, sale items should be priced in even dollar amounts.

By using a quarter as the lowest denomination of your pricing, you will find making change to be much simpler and more efficient. This becomes a real asset in situations where there are several cashiers or many shoppers buying at the same time.

Leave Room For Negotiation

Rarely are prices at garage sales cast in stone. Both buyers and sellers know that some price haggling is part of the game. As a seller, you should set your prices to reflect that fact. Be careful not to set your prices too high, however, or potential buyers may be afraid that a reasonable offer will be insulting and pass the item entirely. On the other hand, don't get upset at a real lowball offer--often shoppers will offer a ridiculous price just to see if you are willing to bargain.

We will discuss bargaining at some length in Chapter 9.

Quantity Discounts

Quantity discounts can be used to advantage when there is a great deal of similar merchandise. If you are selling a quantity of children's clothing in roughly the same sizes, offering one free with every two purchased will help to sell more. Pricing can also reflect a discount--for example, 25 cents each or 5 for a dollar.

NEVER Give Away

This is probably the most important of the "Rules of Thumb"! **NEVER give anything away unless it helps you sell something else.** Have you seen FREE boxes at garage sales? Most people are reluctant to dig in and help themselves and those who do rarely buy anything else. Why not pay customers to take the items you planned to give away? This will make shoppers feel an obligation to purchase something.

At your next sale, set up a "WE'LL PAY YOU TO TAKE THESE" area and pay shoppers a quarter to take each item (set a limit of one per customer). You'll be surprised how much interest this will generate AND how many of the people who let you pay them to take one item end up buying several others. One of the best ways to hold shoppers interest is to do something totally unexpected. Paying them to take away an item will more than pay for itself!

SETTING PRICES

The most important thing to remember when setting prices is that your garage sale is not competing with retail stores or antique shops, it is competing with other garage sales. Garage sale shoppers have a well deserved reputation for being very price conscious. They simply refuse to pay retail prices for merchandise they buy from someone operating in a basement or garage.

If you have taken the time to shop other sales, you should have a pretty good feel for the price people will pay for various types of items. Although it is difficult to offer a suggestion for pricing each item, using a percentage of replacement cost offers a good place to start.

The best quality items offered in a garage sale should bring anywhere from 25 to 35% of their

> *"He ne'er consider'd it, as loth*
> *To look a gift horse*
> *in the mouth"*
> *.....Samuel Butler, 1612-1680*

current replacement cost. Merchandise in fair or poor condition may be hard pressed to bring 10%. The following table will give you some idea of the percentage for various price categories:

Table Of Percentages For Prices From $5.00 To $100.00:

Price	15%	25%	30%	35%
$ 5.00	.75	1.25	1.50	1.75
$10.00	1.50	2.50	3.00	3.50
$15.00	2.25	3.75	4.50	5.25
$20.00	3.00	5.00	6.00	7.00
$25.00	3.75	6.25	7.50	8.75
$30.00	4.50	7.50	9.00	10.50
$35.00	5.25	8.75	10.50	12.25
$40.00	6.00	10.00	12.00	14.00
$45.00	6.75	11.25	13.50	15.75
$50.00	7.50	12.50	15.00	17.50
$55.00	8.25	13.75	16.50	19.25
$60.00	9.00	15.00	18.00	21.00
$65.00	9.75	16.25	19.50	22.75
$70.00	10.50	17.50	21.00	24.50
$75.00	11.25	18.75	22.50	26.25
$80.00	12.00	20.00	24.00	28.00
$85.00	12.75	21.25	25.50	29.75
$90.00	13.50	22.50	27.00	31.50
$95.00	14.25	23.75	28.50	33.25
100.00	15.00	25.00	30.00	35.00

MARKING YOUR ITEMS

Prices need to be clearly marked on every piece of merchandise. Generally it is better to use individual pricing and mark each item so there is absolutely no question as to its' price. It is important to mark the price on each item in a way that will not damage it. In this section we will discuss methods for marking prices and show you some ways of including considerably more information on your price tags.

Price Tags And Labels

There are several common types of tags and labels:

1. Attaching types are held in place by strings, pins, staples or actually pass through the item. Often attaching type labels are used for items of clothing, linens, plush toys, upholstered furniture and fabric craft items.

2. Self-sticking types may be one piece or security labels designed to tear into pieces when removed. This type of label works best on items that have a relatively smooth, hard surface. Labels should be easily seen but not cover up any important selling points of the item to which they are attached. Colored labels or dots are self-sticking and worth the extra few cents they cost.

3. Plain paper labels may be pinned, stapled, taped, glued or otherwise attached to an item. Rubber cement is particularly effective for holding plain paper labels in place on non-fabric items. Residue from the rubber cement rubs away when the label is removed. Plain paper labels are often used for items that require some explanation or use instructions.

4. Pieces of masking tape are often used as price tags. Finding a pen to write on the rough surface without penetrating the backing is a problem. Masking tape is relatively easy to remove, but is also the sloppiest looking way to label your goods. If you must use masking tape, **PLEASE** cut it from the roll neatly rather than just tearing off a chunk!

Some tags and labels are quite permanent, while others are very easily removed. While there is some possibility of shoppers switching labels that are too easily removed, the "never come off" variety can be a real problem to remove.

It is important to be consistent in where you place your labels, particularly on garments. If you put a label in the neck of one shirt, do the same for every shirt. Shoppers will rapidly learn where to look for your labels and very much appreciate the ease with which they can find them.

Any office supply store will have a good selection of tags and labels. If there is no convenient local source of tags and labels, send for the Silver Streak catalog of garage sale materials mentioned on the order blank in the back of this book! You can, of course, improvise and make your own.

Basic Information

The most important piece of information to include on EVERY tag is the price of the item. I have seen a lot of items at garage sales that did not have a price clearly marked. Don't rely on your memory for prices--mark each item clearly.

The second most important piece of information to include is the size, for those items that come in various sizes. You will sell a lot more merchandise if the size is prominently marked on each item. Often the size is indicated on labels in garments or printed elsewhere on other items, but be sure to include size information on your price tag. If you are unable to recall or locate the exact size, put a reasonable guess on the tag. "Worn by a 5-6 year old" or "approx. size 7" is considerably more helpful than no size information at all!.

Measure and include size information for curtains, blinds, tablecloths, blankets, etc. Most shoppers do not carry tape measures (although you should have one handy), so including the size information helps them decide if they will be able to use your item.

Source information should be included on price tags for items when there are multiple sellers. Most often just two initials will do, unless you have several people with the same initials. Devise a coding system so you can identify the seller. Keep your records separated so there will be no question as to who sold how much. We will offer a few suggestions for keeping those records in the chapter on conducting your sale.

Making Your Labels More Informative

You may include a simple statement such as "Like New," "Never Used," "Works Fine" or "Needs Repair" which helps explain the price you are asking for each item. It stands to reason that a new item will fetch more than one that has been heavily used, an item that works is worth more than one that needs repairs, etc. By including this information on price tags, you are doing two very important things:

1. Establishing credibility with your shoppers.

2. Explaining the price in writing so you won't have to answer a lot of questions.

If additional information will help a shopper decide on your items, be sure to include it. Such information could include:

1. Age (purchased last year)

2. Condition

3. Use information (apple peeler, frequency counter, etc.)

4. Repair details (if repairs are needed, where they can be done and approximate cost)

5. Warranty or service contract information

6. Anything else that will help sell the item.

You can also include a price code to indicate the lowest price the seller will accept for that particular item. This information is valuable for sales where there are multiple sellers and they are not available to answer pricing questions during the sale. One of the simplest price codes involves assigning a numeric value to letters, such as A=9, B=8, C=7, D=6, E=5, etc. If your lowest price is $5.00, then a discreet E somewhere on the price tag will indicate that fact to those working the sale.

One Price Codes

Some groups of items can be marked and priced the same. You may post a key to your codes at several prominent sites around your sale. This is especially helpful for smaller items which do not lend themselves to classification or large groups of similar items which can be lumped together. It is still best practice to mark each item individually with either a price or price code.

Price codes can be designated by letters and/or colors. Do not use numbers, since they will be easily confused with dollar amounts. This is a perfect application for the little colored dots you can buy at any office supply store.

The primary advantage to one price codes is the ease with which price adjustments can be made during the sale. Make up several keys for use at various stages of your sale. Have plenty of keys available, prominently displayed and all changed at the same time!

6

INFORMING EVERYONE

All your careful preparations will be for naught if the public is unaware of your sale. **The single most common reason for unsuccessful garage sales is the lack of sufficient advertising.** Look at the need to inform your potential customers as an opportunity, not a problem. Be willing to commit the time and money necessary to do a good job of advertising.

The difference between a well advertised sale and an unadvertised one is readily apparent by the amount of traffic at each. Well advertised sales have shoppers waiting at the door before opening time. In vivid contrast are sales advertised only by a small sign or two around the neighborhood--the few shoppers at these sales are there almost by accident.

NEWSPAPER ADVERTISING

Avid garage sale shoppers study classified ads in the newspaper. Most of the sales in our area start on Thursday. Shoppers check Wednesday papers and make a list of sales they'd like to attend. The most desirable sales are put at the top of their list. The focus of this section will be how to advertise your sale in such a way that it will be at the top of many lists.

Grabbing Attention

Most newspapers have categories for garage, estate, craft sales, bazaars and auctions in their classified advertising section. In most papers during the summer, there are several columns of garage sale classified ads on Wednesday evenings.

Some of the ads catch your eye immediately, others look very routine.

Most sales are listed by city or location, so an ad that starts out with Gigantic, Fantastic, Huge, or Once In A Lifetime really stands out. A heading is the place to be flamboyant and imaginative. If the common practice in your area is to list sales by city or location, put a "teaser" ad--such as "See the best sale in town," "Once in a lifetime bargains"--in that category directing the readers attention to your sale ad elsewhere.

Humor can be an effective attention getting device. You may want to advertise a "Divorce Sale--Prices Split Down The Middle" or "Twenty Years of Being A Packrat Ends." How about something like "Send Our Kids To College Sale" or "Pre Trash Day Clearance?" A little humor can help get your ad noticed.

Be Descriptive

The body of your ad should be descriptive, not excessively wordy. For instance, "A good selection of automotive accessories and woodworking tools will be featured" will not get a lot more attention than "Auto accessories and woodworking tools."

Your ad should compel prospective shoppers to seek you out. A good variety of merchandise, reasonable prices, extra hours, attractions such as baked goods or craft items will help. A general description of the types of merchandise offered will usually suffice, although sizes of clothing should be listed if possible, i.e., "Teen boys and girls clothing" or "Toddler clothes and toys."

Be sure to describe any special circumstances surrounding your sale, particularly if they will give shoppers some reason to stop.   Garage sale shoppers frequent moving and estate sales because there is usually an excellent variety of merchandise at reasonable prices.

Special Item Listing

Be sure to mention any special items in your newspaper ad.   The range of items that can be considered special is wide indeed.   Some of the special items most frequently mentioned are weightlifting sets, Camcorders, stereo equipment, antiques of all kinds, collectibles, Avon bottles, specialty tools, auto parts, tires, office furniture, hobby supplies and cosmetics.

It is safe to assume those items that sell for more than a few dollars are candidates for special listing, particularly if they will help attract more shoppers. As mentioned earlier, baked goods or craft items certainly qualify as special and should be listed as such.

Days And Time

The days (both in day and date) and times your sale will be operation should be clearly stated in

"I keep six honest-serving men
(They taught me all I knew);
Their names are What and Why
and When
and How and Where
and Who"
.....Rudyard Kipling, 1865-1936

your ad. Unorthodox hours or days will attract those shoppers who are unable to shop at more conventional times.

Don't advertise your sale too far in advance of the first day. If your sale is to begin on Thursday, reserve newspaper space for Wednesday. Garage sale shoppers tend to respond to advertising which features sales in the next day or two. Sales advertised more than a few days in advance will only attract a larger group of early birds.

Directions

Unless your sale will be held in a location known to virtually everyone in town, include some simple directions. These need not be elaborate, but should give shoppers at least a general idea of where the sale is located. "1147 E. Prospect St., 1 block south of K-Mart" or "4420 Pinehill Terrace, near Lincoln School" should enable shoppers to find you with relative ease. Many shoppers skip sales because the address is in an obscure part of town or give up in exasperation after several futile attempts to find a specific address.

Phone Number

There are two schools of thought regarding phone numbers in garage sale ads. The advantages are primarily for shoppers, since they can call you with any questions regarding your merchandise. Of course, you will also get some calls from Early Birds. Some contend that including your phone number is an open invitation to distraction during your sale. You will not have much time to spend answering the phone when actually conducting your sale.

It would seem reasonable to include your phone number if you have advertised specialty items. Shoppers appreciate being able to check on them before driving to your sale. If you are offering a broad selection of merchandise, it is best to have shoppers actually visit the sale.

A telephone answering machine can be put to good use during your garage sale. Answer with an announcement concerning your sale and invite the caller to leave a message if there are specific questions. In this way, you will be able to return the important calls at your convenience.

Special Notices

You may also include some special notices in your newspaper ad. Some of the more common ones-- "No Checks," "No Early Sales," "Offers Considered," "Prices Firm" and "Not Responsible For Accidents." If you want to attract more attention (and shoppers), you might want to try notices such as "Anything You Ever Wanted To Buy," or "If We Don't Have It, You Don't Want It." How about "High Class Junque" or "Worth A Trip From Anywhere ?"

Don't Scrimp

Newspaper advertising may seem expensive, but it's false economy to scrimp on your ads. The most common method of trying to save money is abbreviating excessively. Too many abbreviations leave the impression that your sale is not worth the price of the ad. Would you be interested in a garage sale whose ad read "BETT. THURS., FRI., SAT Hsehld, toys, misc. 8-5. 1400 Elm St.?"

Another temptation is to make your sale advertisement too brief. In a long column of sale ads, something must be different to make yours stand out. If most ads are 2 or 3 lines long, make yours 5 or 6. Ask the newspaper to put a special logo at the top, outline the ad with a bold box, use large print for the headings or add some distinctive feature to make your advertisement stand out from the crowd.

Rather than spending extra money to run your ad for a week before the sale, use that money to run a larger ad for only a few days. After all, you are interested in attracting the shoppers attention and must use every trick to do so.

Other Papers

So far, we have concentrated on major newspapers in your area. While it is important to hit the major papers with your sale advertisement, some creative looking will probably reveal several more publications are effective places to advertise. Many areas have small weekly newspapers and free distribution "Shoppers" that are regularly read by avid garage sale shoppers. Since the cost for advertising in these publications is usually considerably less than the major newspapers, consider using them whenever possible.

> *"Half the money I spend on
> advertising is wasted,
> and the trouble is
> I don't know which half."
> ...Viscount Leverhulme,
> 1851-1925*

SIGNS

Signs are critical to the success of any garage sale. Signs attract attention, direct shoppers to a sale and to provide information at the sale. After the first day or so, signs are the way that 95% of your shoppers will learn about your sale!

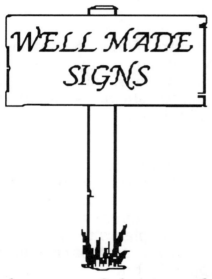

Remember the 9 X 12 cardboard sign done in #3 pencil that we mentioned in the first chapter? Let's agree right now that you would never, ever use that type of sign for any sale in which you are involved!

Placement

Signs must always be placed where they will be of most assistance to your shoppers. Sale signs, for example, should be posted prominently on traffic routes and guide shoppers to your sale. Take a drive around the vicinity and decide where the best possible locations for your signs will be. Plan for arrows pointing in the proper direction, and remember the arrows on two sided signs will need to point in the same direction. Make a map of the locations you have selected and some notes as to what size and type of sign will be most effective.

As an experiment, we decided to hold a garage sale with no other advertising than a couple of large signs posted at busy intersections in the immediate vicinity of our house. We placed the signs early on a Saturday morning. No sooner had the signs been placed than we were flooded with shoppers and had one of our best sales. Had smaller signs been placed on less busy streets, the sale would not have been nearly as successful!

Many sale signs are tacked to utility poles, traffic light supports or existing sign posts. This is a dangerous (and in many areas, illegal) practice. It is far better to make your signs freestanding and place them well away from utility poles and traffic signs. Get permission from the property owner so signs can be anchored to the ground with a stake or tripod. Sign frames, such as those used by Realtors, may be used to hold garage sale signs.

Signs to be used at the sale location should be posted where they will be most effective. Information about merchandise should be located near that merchandise, general sale rules at the entrance and expressions of gratitude at the exit. Try to keep signs at eye level and in plain sight.

Getting Noticed

The best sign in the world will do no good if people never notice it. Making sure your sale signs get noticed requires a lot of creativity. The size of lettering on a sign goes a long way in determining whether or not it gets noticed. As a general rule, bigger is better when it comes to signs and lettering size.

Creative use of color will help get your signs noticed. This past summer we saw a lot of garage sale signs in neon green, yellow and orange. With printing in a strongly contrasting color, the neon signs are real attention getters.

Attaching things to your signs helps attract attention. Pennants, balloons, pinwheels, flashing lights and tinsel are commonly used. Balloons offer a couple of advantages--they move around in the wind, are colorful and cheap enough to use in quantity on all your signs.

Information

The amount and type of information to be included on each sign depends entirely on signs function. One of the most important principles of the advertising world is **KISS,** which stands for **Keep It Short & Simple!** Keep this principle in mind when planning your signs and make them simple as possible. Use only as many words as absolutely necessary to convey your message. Don't gussy up your signs with a lot of extraneous decoration. Pick a color scheme and use it consistently. Have someone else read each sign to see if you agree on what it is trying to say.

Some of the most effective signs have only the word SALE and an arrow pointing in the right direction. A little way down the street another sign with a few more details can be posted. Be sure all your signs are the same color and style so the drivers know they are stalking the right sale.

If you recall the Burma Shave signs used years ago, the amount of information to put on each sign was well illustrated. Each of the signs consisted of only a few words, but a series of signs comprised a jingle and mentioned Burma Shave. Your sale can be very effectively advertised using this same idea. Try making a series of short statements regarding your sale and put them on sequential signs. How about something like "SHOP OUR SALE," "AND SAVE SOME MONEY," "LOTS OF TOYS," "FOR YOUR LITTLE HONEY," "1910 Elm Street?"

Shoppers appreciate original and creative signs. There are many ways to say the same thing. For example, you might want to say that you will not accept checks. You could say "NO CHECKS" or "CASH ONLY." A more creative approach might be to say "CHECKS CASHED AT FIRST NATIONAL, 6 BLOCKS WEST" or "WE'LL

HOLD YOUR PURCHASE UNTIL THE CHECK CLEARS." How about "IN GOD WE TRUST, ALL OTHERS PAY CASH?"

Don't post a lot of nasty signs. You know the type--"NO CHECKS," "NO CHILDREN," "NOT RESPONSIBLE FOR ACCIDENTS," "DO NOT OPEN PACKAGES," "PRICES ARE FIRM" and "YOU BREAK IT, YOU BUY IT." The messages conveyed by these signs may be legitimate, but the tone will certainly offend most shoppers. Can you think of some nice ways to say the same thing? Re-read the last paragraph to find some examples of creativity and apply them to your own nasty signs. Try to convey the message, be creative and leave your shoppers with a good feeling rather than resentment.

Consider Drivers

One of the most frequent problems with garage sale signs is that they are impossible to read from a moving car. Perhaps some drivers can read fine print at 35 miles per hour, but the vast majority don't even try. If you are going to post a sign and expect drivers to notice and read it, try driving by it yourself to see how well you did. Remember one of the most effective signs mentioned a few paragraphs ago--"SALE" with a large arrow?

If you drive around to other sales on a weekend, pay particular attention to the types of signs most easily read from a moving car. Look for some that are difficult to read and see why. A picture, as they say, is worth a thousand words. Seeing for yourself will quickly give you the picture regarding signs that are most effective.

Making Signs

Everyone knows how to make signs, right? That may well be true, but here are a few suggestions your signs:

1. Use good quality material for the background. Posterboard does well for interior signs, tempered hardboard or plywood for outdoor use. Posterboard can be purchased in many colors, including some of the bright new neon shades. Hardboard is tannish brown in color, plywood is lighter. Either can be easily painted to make a light colored background.

2. Lettering should be big, bold and bright! Paint the letters or use permanent marking pens. Avoid the temptation to put too much information on a sign and make the lettering considerably larger than you think is necessary.

3. If you are not good at freehand lettering, use commercially available patterns or stencils.

If your signs are to be used outdoors, protect them in one of the following ways:

1. Use a clear plastic self-stick material such as Contact Paper.

2. Cover the surface of the sign with clear plastic sheeting and tape it securely.

3. Spray the sign liberally with aerosol waterproof coating.

4. If you have no other means, put the sign in a gigantic plastic bag (clear, of course) and seal it that way.

Assume it will rain for at least one of the days of your sale and protect your signs accordingly

Wind is another element that creates problems with garage sale signs. Signs that buckle and flap in the breeze are impossible to read. Signs that are sturdy and securely anchored will not be unduly affected by the wind.

Signs may be supported in several ways. They can be attached to an existing structure (with the owner's permission, of course) or free standing. Using sandwich board type construction, a sign can be self supporting and needs only to be anchored to the ground. Using supports driven into the ground will also work well. If your sign is over a foot square, supports attached to either end will work much better than a single one in the middle.

Remember that you want your signs to last for the duration of your sale, so make and support them with that in mind. Your signs will make an immediate impression on potential shoppers who read them. **Most people assume that sloppy, poorly planned signs lead to a sloppy, poorly planned sale.** Signs can be used repeatedly, so don't neglect to make them right the first time.

Buying Signs

Some of the signs you need can be purchased at hardware or office supply stores. Most have an area to fill in your address or other information. Self-stick letters in various colors are available, but somewhat costly.

If you see some signs at a sale that look like they might work for yours, why not offer to buy them at the end of the sale? Owners with no plans for another sale in the near future are often willing to sell their signs.

In some areas, you can rent signs. Usually mounted on trailers, these signs feature bold lettering and often include flashing lights or other attention getting devices. If you are going to have a large sale and can afford to rent this type of sign, by all means do so. The extra attention it attracts will justify the extra expense. Don't forget you will have to negotiate a place to park the sign, unless you plan to keep it on your own property.

OTHER ADVERTISING

In addition to the newspaper ads and signs already discussed, there are several other ways to get the word out about your sale.

Posters

If you or your children are a little artistic, making posters for your sale can be a fun family project. List the information to be included on the posters, supply the materials and let your kids have at it! If you do them yourself, be sure to make the posters interesting and heavy on eye appeal. Post them around town wherever pedestrian traffic is heaviest. Your favorite supermarket may have an area you can use. Other retail stores, laundromats, restaurants and clubs frequently provide bulletin boards for the use of their customers. You'll be amazed how effective posters can be in creating interest in your sale.

Handouts, Flyers

A couple of weeks prior to your sale prepare a handout describing all the details and distribute copies to your neighbors, relatives and friends. In addition to providing potential customers, your handout should invite anyone interested in participating to contact you. Perhaps one or more of those you contact will decide to have a sale at the same time or contribute merchandise to yours.

Prepare another flyer describing your sale, send it to friends and relatives who might be interested in any of the merchandise you will be offering. If you know of anyone who will be holding a sale at the same time as yours, arrange for them to distribute your flyers in exchange for your distributing theirs. Remember the shopping mall effect we talked about earlier? More sales generate more excitement among shoppers.

Word Of Mouth

One of the most effective and inexpensive forms of advertising is word of mouth. Pass the word regarding your sale at every opportunity. Inform your friends and ask them to tell their friends. The more people who know about your sale, the better. If you have merchandise that you know will interest someone in particular, why not let them know directly?

Freebies

There are many ways to get free publicity for your sale. One of the most effective is to arrange to donate a percentage of the proceeds to a church or social group to which you belong. In addition to providing a pool of potential customers or sale participants, the group will often advertise your sale in whatever newsletter it publishes. Of course, you will get additional exposure at group gatherings and possibly some mention in the local media. The amount you donate can usually be deducted from your income taxes as a charitable contribution.

Some radio and television stations provide a call-in or post card program for people to advertise merchandise for sale, trade or give-away. These programs are a good garage sale advertising medium and almost always are either free or very inexpensive. The rules for participation vary from station to station and are usually announced at the beginning of each program.

As we said at the beginning of this chapter, you must make the public aware of your sale. Anything you can do to attract shoppers will make a significant difference in the amount of money your sale brings in.

Never underestimate the power of advertising!

7

LADDERS

TABLES

SAW HORSES

DISPLAYING YOUR MERCHANDISE

The purpose of a good display is to make shoppers stop, look and buy merchandise. In other words, **display** helps create **demand**. As evidenced by the amount of time and money devoted to displays in retail stores, it takes a great deal of thought and creativity to set up displays that properly motivate shoppers.

We've all seen the stereotype image of garage sale merchandise display--dump all the goods on a table in a dingy garage, put the clothes in piles and drop a few items in the driveway. Be sure everything is covered in a layer of dust and grime. Ever wonder why it takes a very motivated shopper to dig for things they would like to buy from that type of display? Would you buy things displayed in that fashion?

One of the most important things you can do prior to setting up your own sale is to spend some time at a shopping mall. Look at the displays in each store and ask yourself these questions:

1. How are they set up?

2. What kind of message do they convey?

3. Do they make you interested in the merchandise on display?

4. How could you make the display more interesting to you?

5. What other kinds of merchandise could be displayed in the same fashion?

6. Does the display make it easy for you to buy the merchandise?

7. Where can you get more information about the items on display?

Importance Of Good Display

One of the primary purposes of effective garage sale display is to get potential customers to stop and get out of their cars. As the old saying goes,, "You never get a second chance to make a first impression." Shoppers need to see enough merchandise, anything that arouses curiosity or something distinctive that makes the effort of leaving their cars worthwhile.

Once customers have stopped at your sale, the effectiveness of your display techniques will, in large part, determine the prices your merchandise will bring. Shoddy merchandise poorly displayed will not bring anywhere near the prices of properly displayed good merchandise.

There is a cumulative effect in garage sales, just as there is at a shopping mall. Having enough good merchandise well displayed will help each individual item sell better. The more you have, the more you will sell. Shoppers like to see a lot of merchandise in one place and will spend more time browsing than if there are just a few items scattered around on tables.

> *"It's better to be looked over than overlooked."*
> *...Mae West, 1892-1980*

DISPLAY AREAS

While you can scatter merchandise randomly throughout the sale area, there are several types of items that lend themselves to separate display areas:

Toys

Kids toys have been mentioned several times in preceding chapters, but are important enough to merit special attention here. Set toys aside in a special area out of the general traffic flow. Be sure to display your items at children's eye level and make the display fun and attractive for kids. By enclosing the toy area, you can help your sale by keeping the kids busy while their parents shop. Often children will find a toy to which they become very attached while Mom and Dad are shopping elsewhere. Most often, the parents will end up buying a toy or two.

Don't forget that toys are often purchased as gifts by grandparents and others. At our house, we have a large box of garage sale toys for the grandchildren to play with and then take home with them. Grandma and Grandpa have a great deal of fun replacing the toys at garage sales and the children love to get more toys when they come to visit.

Clearly label each toy not only by price, but also by the age group for which it is appropriate. Baby toys should be displayed with any other baby items you have to sell.

Clothes

Clothes, if you have enough, certainly warrant a separate display area. Be sure to have each item clean, sized and priced clearly. Group men, women and children's clothing separately and identify each group with a sign. You will sell a lot more clothes if you keep similar sized items together. Often a shopper will buy several items of clothing to fit the same person--keeping sizes together encourages this type of purchasing.

As mentioned earlier, the best way to display most clothing items is on hangers. Things not normally hung on hangers can be easily attached to a hanger with small safety pins. Displaying your clothing on hangers offers three distinct advantages:

1. Shoppers can easily examine the garment.

2. Clothes do not wrinkle nearly as much on hangers.

3. You are not faced with the task of re-folding and stacking clothing displayed on a table.

Use backgrounds to display special items. If possible, provide a small private place to try on clothes. There are many fixtures you can use to display clothing, as we will discuss a little later in this chapter.

Furniture

Furniture should be displayed in a relatively open space where customers can try it and removal is easy. Display related items in groups with any accessories you may have for sale. For example, you could display a tablecloth, candle holders and nice china with a dining room set. The accessories will help sell the larger item and, if priced separately, will often sell with it. Be sure each of your items is cleaned and polished as much as possible.

Large Appliances

Large appliances, such as refrigerators or freezers, should be left plugged in to demonstrate to shoppers that they work. Also, the interior light will help show the appliance to best advantage. Have a power cord available so shoppers can try other types of appliances that would not be practical to operate full time during the sale (such as space heaters, air conditioners or dehumidifiers.)

Use an appliance cleaner and wax to help restore the shiny surfaces everyone likes to see. Chips in the finish can be easily remedied with touch-up materials available at any appliance store. Be sure your appliances are squeaky clean, including the back and sides!

Hanging Things

Pictures, clocks, mirrors, light fixtures and other items that usually hang from walls or ceilings should be hung on the background or suspended at their usual height. If the item is a light fixture, try to have it operating. Be sure pictures and decorative items are clean and have plenty of light so they can be readily seen. Clocks should be wound, plugged in or have a fresh battery so they can operate. Mirrors can be displayed in such a way that they will help you see all around the sale area. Try to have most hanging things displayed at eye level so shoppers can visualize how the items will look in their own home.

Automotive Items And Tools

Automotive items and tools should be set aside in a special area out of the general traffic flow, since men will often spend time looking in this area while the ladies are shopping the rest of the sale. Provide power to try electric tools and signs explaining the features of any uncommon items.

Be sure all your tools are as clean and grease free as possible. A few minutes spent cleaning, sharpening and repairing tools will pay big dividends in their salability.

Baby Items

Baby furniture, clothes, toys and related items should be grouped in one area. Be sure to include any items which could be used as baby gifts, such as stuffed animals. If you have maternity clothes, include them in the same area or provide signs indicating where they can be found. Similarly, signs pointing out the baby goods should be put in the maternity clothes area.

Any especially cute baby items should be featured by displaying them on the background. Be sure they are well lighted. Sprinkle a little baby powder in the clothes and furniture--shoppers like to buy things that smell like babies.

Electronics

If you have a quantity of electronic items to sell, it is wise to set them in a separate area. Have power available and put fresh batteries in those items that need them (and work, of course). For non-working items, indicate the problem and repair cost, if known. Try to demonstrate or explain with a sign any item that is unusual. Display related items such as records, tapes, CD's, video tapes, etc., in the same area.

Kitchen Appliances And Gadgets

Kitchen appliances and gadgets are the mainstay of most garage sales and, as such, deserve special attention as to the way they're displayed. Since some of the items may be unfamiliar to shoppers, be sure to provide instruction books, original boxes or a sign indicating how they work.

Remember that power may be required to try some of the appliances. Display any closely related items together. Be sure that all items are as clean and shiny as possible.

Sporting Goods

This diverse group of items may need to be displayed in any of several ways. Firearms MUST be unloaded and kept far out of the reach of children. Sized items should be near a place where they can be tried. Provide enough room to try and some advice on how to use things that may be suitable for beginners in a particular sport.

Small Items

There are hundreds of miscellaneous small items in most garage sales, ranging from cameras to jewelry. While it would be impossible to describe exactly how to display each type of item, here are some general guidelines:

1. Be sure your items are in plain sight of both you and your shoppers to prevent pilfering.

2. If necessary, display cases may be used. Several types of display cases will be described in the section on fixtures.

3. Jewelry may be displayed in divided plastic boxes or egg cartons.

4. All small items should be well lighted and displayed at different levels.

5. Avoid the temptation to just dump small items on a table!

The Non-Display

Remember the "Ask To See" signs we mentioned in an earlier chapter? Since most shoppers won't bother to ask, why not set up a display area for those items that does not allow shoppers direct access? You could use a separate room or area closed off by ropes. Interested shoppers could be let in to examine the items. Use some signs making shoppers aware of the display and post a positive sign like "We'll be happy to show you these items" at the point where entrance is restricted.

DISPLAY FIXTURES

An infinite variety of things may be used as display fixtures for a garage sale. If you are flexible and creative, many common household items can be used as displays. You must be willing to spend a few dollars to make your sale displays attractive and functional--in the long run you will realize considerably more profit.

Tables

For many types of merchandise, tables are a good display fixture. Try to get a few of the sturdy folding type commonly used at schools, churches or social clubs. Most of these are about 6 feet long and close to 3 feet wide. Many rental stores offer these tables at a very reasonable price.

You can make your own tables using saw horses for legs and sturdy plywood or wooden doors for tops. Card tables, picnic tables or large TV tray tables may also be pressed into display service. Avoid light weight folding tables if possible--they bend under the weight of a heavy display or someone inadvertently leaning on them.

Whatever type of table you use, cover the top with a light colored paper or fabric. Long rolls of table covering can be purchased at food supply or discount stores. Using a lighter color will help display your merchandise to good advantage and serve as a light reflector for whatever illumination you are able to provide.

Racks

As mentioned repeatedly throughout this book, the best way to display most clothing is on hangers. There are many types of clothes racks you can use for your sale--none of which are expensive to assemble. Before your garage sale, look around the neighborhood to see if you can borrow a suitable rack. Check your neighborhood rental store to see what kinds of clothing racks are available.

If you can't locate a suitable rack, here are six possibilities:

1. Use galvanized pipe and standardized fittings available at most any hardware store. It is quite easy to construct a rack supported by some other structure (like a door frame or wall), or freestanding.

2. Hang a wooden or aluminum ladder from the ceiling or suspend the ladder between two step ladders. Be sure to use a sturdy rope or step ladders if you try this!

3. Hang a sturdy wooden dowel from ceiling joists with a rope. Again, be sure both the rope and the dowel are sufficiently strong for the task.

4. Mount two closet support brackets on the wall and use a standard closet size rod.

5. Use a step ladder with a rope or rod between the legs.

6. If you have just a few clothes, you could hang them on a clothes line. For those items you feel need more exposure, hang them with clothespins just like you do on washday.

Shelves

An old bookcase or set of steel storage shelves can be turned into a very functional display fixture. As an alternative, you can use lightweight plastic "snap-together" shelves, but limit the amount of weight you try to put on them. Tipping can be a problem with lightweight shelves, so put heavier items on the bottom shelves.

You can make your own shelves using cement blocks for supports and boards for the actual shelves. If your shelving span will be over three feet, put a cement block support in the center.

Shelves may be constructed using sturdy cardboard boxes of different sizes. Tape the box lids closed, then tape the boxes together. By putting larger boxes on the bottom, then stacking smaller boxes on top, you can make surprisingly sturdy shelves. To make your shelves even sturdier, fill the boxes with Styrofoam pellets or other packing material prior to taping them shut.

There are many paper or self-stick vinyl shelf coverings available to cover your shelves. You can also use fabrics, which are particularly effective for displaying more costly merchandise. Be sure to choose a light color and tape them down to prevent the entire cover from being pulled off accidentally.

Display Cases

Some kinds of merchandise should be displayed in a closed front case to prevent shoppers from handling or pocketing them. Perhaps you will be lucky enough to have some type of display case available. If not, here are a few ways you can construct your own:

1. Use a sturdy cardboard or wooden box and replace the bottom with Plexiglas or shrink-fit plastic. By laying the box on its' side, you can use the bottom for viewing and the top for access.

2. Small items can be effectively displayed in egg carton type boxes or dividers surrounded by a frame and covered with Plexiglas. This type of display case can be built very inexpensively.

3. If you have a lot of items to display, cover the front and sides of a storage shelf unit and access it from the rear. Using the shrink-fit plastic sold for window coverings allows clear visibility and protection for your merchandise.

4. For open display cases, use divided plastic boxes or fishing tackle boxes available at most discount stores. If you need a covered case, assemble as many of these boxes as you need and cut a piece of Plexiglas to fit over them all.

Boxes

Sturdy cardboard boxes can be used as display bins. Cut off the top of the box and slope the sides so the tallest portion is in the rear and the shortest at the front. Many small items can be displayed in these makeshift bins. Items displayed in bins should be individually marked, but these modified boxes provide an excellent means of separating groups of items by price.

If you have the original boxes for some of your sale items, use them as part of the display. Most boxes have a picture of the item, list of some of the features and sometimes still have the original price marked on them. You can usually get a considerably better price for an item displayed in its original box.

One very effective display fixture is a large appliance box (refrigerator, water heater, etc.) available from any appliance store. These boxes are very sturdy and can be used for pinning lightweight items on all four sides. Put a foot or so of sand in the bottom and tape the top closed. You can cover the sides with a background of paper or fabric and have an excellent fixture for almost no cost. If you are unable to find a box, use 2 x 8 pieces of tempered hardboard, plywood or pegboard assembled in the shape of a rectangular box.

Hanging Fixtures

Some merchandise can be best displayed hanging from the ceiling or wall. On the wall, pegboard with associated hangers works very well. You can also use plain plywood with cup hooks or thumbtacks. Thin 4 x 8 sheets of Styrofoam can be attached to existing walls and used to display merchandise hung on small nails or cup hooks. Large sheets of cardboard can also be attached to existing walls and used in the same fashion. If you would rather not attach plywood, Styrofoam or cardboard to existing walls, use a sheet of whatever type of material you have available., Attach a leg on either side for support, forming a tripod to set on a table or the floor.

Large hooks or nails in the wall will allow you to hang heavy pictures, mirrors, etc. Bicycle hooks in the ceiling or rafters will provide hanging capability for light fixtures or other items that need a lot of hanging room.

Specialty Fixtures

You can use a standing ladder (properly supported, of course) to display linens, towels, shoes, boots, etc. It is quite easy to construct a multipurpose rack that resembles a standing ladder supported by two wooden feet using 1 x 6 sides, 1 x 1 cross pieces and 2 x 4 feet. By alternating the cross pieces, the fixture can be used for shoes and boots. Putting the cross pieces directly across from each other sets the rack up for other types of items.

You may be lucky enough to have an old display fixture or two available for your sale. Look around at store closing sales and other garage sales for specialty display fixtures that can be renovated with a little polish and paint. A small investment in fixtures can make your garage sale look much more professional and make your merchandise displays considerably easier to assemble.

Be Creative And Flexible

If you look carefully around your house, you will find with many items that can be used as display fixtures.   With a little creativity and imagination, you can design displays that are attractive and functional.

8

GARAGE SALE

BOOKS

$10.00

CONDUCTING YOUR SALE

Let's assume that you have selected, priced and displayed all your merchandise. The advertising has been done and the signs are ready. You are about to launch your sale. This chapter will help you through the actual sale itself. We will be concentrating on a few last minute details, some practical sales techniques and other skills you will need to conduct the sale successfully.

LAST MINUTE PREPARATIONS

There are some details best left until just prior to the sale. If all your merchandise is in place and ready, there will be just a few last minute things to take care of.

Cash Box And Change

Hopefully, you have a suitable cash box. Boxes designed to hold cash are available at office supply stores or by mail order (send for the Silver Streak Garage Sale Supplies Catalog). Alternately, a divided fishing tackle or sewing box can be used. Ideally, there should be a separate compartment for each common denomination of coins (5, 10, 25, 50 cents) and space for 1, 5, 10 and 20 dollar bills.

To start, you must have an adequate supply of

> *'Nothing astonishes men*
> *so much as*
> *common sense and*
> *plain dealing'*
> *.....R. W. Emerson, 1803-1882*

change. For most sales 2 rolls of each of the coin denominations, 20 one dollar bills, 5 five's, 2 tens and 1 twenty should prove adequate. If your sale is successful, you will need to make change for a lot of shoppers in a very short period of time. Running out of change can be frustrating.

For a multiple day sale, evaluate your change situation at the end of the first day and start out with the same amount of change each succeeding day. If you end up with a lot of extra change, your bank will convert it to bills for you.

It is important that you not keep excess money in your cash box. If you find the box is getting too full, remove and store the excess in a safe place.

Records, Receipts, Forms

Keep some simple records of the prices received for major items. These records will be of assistance in deciding what prices to charge at future sales and give you a running idea of how much money you are making.

If you have multiple sellers, keep records to indicate how much merchandise each one sells. There are several methods of accomplishing this task:

1. Use a notebook or ring binder with a separate page for each seller. Write the amount of each sale on the appropriate page.

2. Use a bulletin board, divided into sections for each seller. Remove the price tag from each

item sold and stick it into the correct section of the board.

3. Use color coded price tags for each separate seller and place all the price tags in a box at the check out. After the sale, it is a simple matter to separate the tags by color.

4. Have each seller prepare a list of his major items, providing a blank for the price received. Enter the correct figures as each item is sold.

As you may have guessed, some of these methods are cumbersome and can bog down the efficiency of your check out station. If possible, have someone keep track of the sales separately while the cashier is concentrating on serving customers efficiently.

You will need a pad of receipts for those customers who request some documentation of their purchase. Inexpensive receipt pads can be purchased at any discount or office supply store.

A convenience for customers is a pre-printed note sheet indicating your name, address and phone number. Leave enough room for them to write information about any item in which they are interested. For those who want to look around or think about an item, these note sheets can mean the difference between making the sale and missing it.

Calculator

By all means, provide a calculator at the check out station. A printing calculator will enable you to offer shoppers a tape receipt for items purchased. It is difficult for a cashier to total items, take care of bagging, record purchases and make change all at the same time. A calculator will ease at least one of those burdens.

Bags, Boxes

One of the most frequent shortcomings of garage sales is the lack of bags or boxes for carrying items purchased. These need not be elaborate--those received with your grocery purchases should do just fine. If you have not saved enough bags and boxes, they can be purchased at office supply or wholesale food outlets. Check with your neighborhood supermarket--they may be glad to sell you enough bags for your sale (and receive some free advertising in return.)

Toward the end of your sale, you can use bags for promotional purposes. Offer selected merchandise at a single price for everything the shopper can fit in a bag. This type of promotion works exceptionally well for clothing and small miscellaneous items. Who can resist the temptation to buy a whole bag of clothes for a dollar or two? You can also bag up some merchandise, staple the bag closed and offer "grab bags" for a very reasonable price.

> *"There is really no such thing as*
> *bad weather,*
> *only different kinds*
> *of good weather"*
> *.....John Ruskin, 1819-1900*

Rain Covers

You should have covers available for any merchandise displayed outside in the (unlikely?) event of rain. Inexpensive plastic sheets can be purchased at any discount or hardware store. Use of these covers demonstrates to your shoppers that you are concerned about the condition of your merchandise. Of course, you can also move merchandise indoors if the weather is unfavorable and you have the extra space.

Fans And Heaters

Basic creature comforts often call for the use of fans or supplementary heaters. Arrange to have them available so your shoppers (and you) will be as comfortable as possible. Heaters consume a great deal of power, so be sure your electrical circuits are capable of handling the extra load.

Place fans or heaters well out of the reach of children and be sure that all safeguards and shields are intact.

Background Music

Providing some soft background music helps your customers to converse with each other privately and creates a relaxing atmosphere in which to shop. Of course, you can use some electronic item you have for sale to provide the music. Just keep an alternate music source handy for when your display item is sold.

Parking

Since you hope to have a lot of traffic, make arrangements for parking in the vicinity of your sale. Use signs, if necessary, to direct shoppers where and where not to park. It is a good idea to let your neighbors know what is happening and to place "No Parking" signs in areas where they may object to your shoppers parking.

If parking is limited in the immediate vicinity of your sale, be sure to indicate with signs where overflow parking is available. Most shoppers will not object to walking a block or two IF they know where parking is available. Block off a parking space close to the door for use as a loading area for customers who have purchased bulky items.

Sign Making And Price Marking Equipment

Have some extra sign materials and permanent markers readily available during your sale. Almost always there are signs that should have been made or need to be changed at the last minute. As your sale progresses, you may want to post additional signs that you may not have made in advance.

Price tags and marking equipment should also be at hand all through your sale. You may want to change prices on some of your items and replace any tags that get damaged. It is far more convenient to have the necessary materials at hand than to have to spend extra time rounding them up.

DAY OF SALE

The opening day of your sale is the culmination of all your planning and preparation. If you have followed the steps outlined so far in this book, your garage sale should be well organized and ready to begin.

Early Birds

No matter how early or late you decide to open your sale, there are always a few shoppers who try to get in to look around before you are ready to open. Often they will use some excuse about not being available during the sale hours, just passing through the neighborhood, etc. In addition to disrupting your last minute preparations, early birds often pick up just the prime merchandise and make a shambles of your displays. On the other hand, we have sold a lot of merchandise to early shoppers at some of our sales.

While you are free to do as you like, many people insist that everyone wait until the advertised hour to shop at their sales. This gives all shoppers the same advantage and lets you finish last minute preparations uninterrupted.

Open On Time

If your advertising has been effective, there will probably be shoppers waiting at the door for your sale to begin. Be sure to open at the advertised time unless there is some compelling reason to start earlier. We mentioned the importance of adhering to the advertised hours earlier, but it bears repeating here. Avid shoppers will be making a circuit of several sales and will have yours somewhere on their schedule. If you happen to be first or last on their lists, sticking closely to the advertised hours of operation could well make a significant difference in the amount of merchandise you sell.

Sales Skills

Before you can sell much merchandise, whether you are operating a garage sale or Bloomingdales, you must sell yourself. **Selling yourself means projecting an image that makes people want to do business with you**. Professional sales people have known this for years and spend as much time selling themselves as their products.   Think of some salespeople you've encountered over the years--why did you willingly buy from some and shy away from doing business with others? Try to put yourself in your customers shoes and visualize what you could do to make him want to buy from you.

Here are some simple ways to sell yourself:

1. Let the customer know you're glad he came.

2. Be interested, alert and friendly. Avoid the artificial gushy type of friendly and simply be yourself.

3. Make small talk with your customers.

4. Accept constructive criticism of your sale and merchandise with tact.

5. Provide for children, rather than restricting their movement to an occasional twitch.

> *"Everyone lives by*
> *selling something"*
> *.....Robert Louis Stevenson,*
> *1850-1894*

6. Be honest as to age, condition, price, repair history and any other knowledge you may have about a particular item you're offering for sale.

7. Be helpful--offer to measure, unfold, move and demonstrate your merchandise.

8. If necessary, help shoppers load merchandise in their cars or arrange for moving bulky items.

Have fun! Let your customers know that you are really enjoying the sale. Don't be afraid to accept and offer a little good-natured kidding. Don't take yourself or your sale too seriously. Some sales are set to a theme and those conducting the sale dress to reflect that theme. If is hard not to have fun if you and your helpers are all dressed like circus clowns or square dancers!

Remember you are there for one single purpose--**to sell merchandise.** Be willing to do whatever it takes to accomplish that goal. Enthusiasm is contagious. The more you can get your shoppers wrapped up in your sale, the more merchandise they will buy!

Don't Do

Shoppers are often amazed at the lack of basic sales skills displayed at many sales. Perhaps the

---

"Mix a little foolishness with your
serious plans:
It's lovely to be silly at the right
moment"
.....Horace, 65-8 BC

best way to illustrate this is to describe some of the problems that have been called to our attention.

Often those conducting the sale have been so engrossed in visiting with each other, drinking coffee (or other beverages), watching TV, reading the newspaper, eating lunch or doing crafts they have failed to notice a customer present and feeling neglected. It is easy for potential customers to slip away from a sale without buying when nobody bothers to notice or acknowledge them.

Craft salespeople are often so involved in demonstrating their craft or describing it in great detail to one customer that others get tired of waiting in line and leave without buying anything.

Being argumentative is a real turn-off to potential customers. A shopper pointing out that a particular piece of merchandise is dirty, broken or defective is really indicating an interest in that item. Most of the time complaints are an unsubtle way of getting a better price on an item. Rather than argue, why not negotiate and get rid of it?

Another method of conducting a sale is to simply sit at the cashier's station and neither greet nor acknowledge customers until they hand over a piece of merchandise. Even a grudging "Thank You" seems difficult for these types. A

> *"The customer is never wrong."*
> *...Cesar Ritz, 1850-1918*

local newspaper columnist recently wrote of attending a sale at which the only person in evidence was sound asleep, roused only occasionally to brush a pesky fly off his nose!

Bargaining

You may safely assume that most customers will try to bargain with you. No matter how reasonable the price, there will always be customers who wants to buy for less. As a matter of fact, price bargaining provides some of the most amusing moments in any garage sale. While it is impossible to tell you how to handle price negotiations, a few rules of thumb may help:

1. Don't bargain for nickels and dimes. If you have set what you consider to be reasonable prices on the small items, stick to your marked prices unless the customer is willing to buy a quantity of similar items.

2. Larger items should be overpriced just a little to allow for price bargaining. Most shoppers expect you to come down from your marked price at least a little, so build some padding into your asking prices.

3. As an alternative to reducing the price, you may offer to include a related item at no charge. This works particularly well where the related item will probably not sell on its own anyway.

> *"Necessity never made*
> *a good bargain"*
> *.....Benjamin Franklin, 1706-1790*

4. Consider both the time of day and the time remaining in your sale when price bargaining. Shoppers are well aware of the fact that prices get considerably more flexible toward the end of a sale. In fact, many of them make a habit of shopping sales late on the final day in hopes of getting good bargains.

5. Be diplomatic with potential customers. Try not to take this bargaining business too seriously. Most shoppers regard price bargaining as a game--you should too!

Phases Of Sales

The first day of any sale is a time of great enthusiasm for both buyers and sellers. Early shoppers are looking for specific pieces of merchandise at favorable prices. On the first day, much of the merchandise that shoppers see as bargains will sell. Most sales will be at or close to the marked price, unless the seller invites price negotiations.

The second day can drag, particularly if a lot of prime merchandise sold the first day. This is an excellent time to regroup your displays and reduce prices. Shoppers will be more price conscious and very likely to want to bargain for every item.

> *"A diplomat...is a person who can tell you to go to hell in such a way that you will actually look forward to the trip."*
> *...Caskie Stinnett, 1911--*

The final day is the time to pull out the stops and sell all your remaining merchandise. You can make across the board price cuts, post signs saying you are open to offers or just sit back and see what happens. Bargain hunters are out in force during the final hours of any sale. Occasionally you will receive an offer to purchase all the remaining merchandise. If the price seems reasonable and you want to clear the place, accept the offer. The final day is also the time to call anyone who has made a written offer on any of your remaining merchandise. If they are still interested, you might be able to sell a few more items.

Arrange For Help

It is not practical to try to run a garage sale single-handedly. You will need to have one person stationed at the check out area and another to help shoppers in the display areas. If you can arrange for more than one extra person, so much the better.

Some neighbors or friends may be willing to help with your sale. If not, call your local high school or college and ask for some names of dependable people you could hire for a few days. As an alternative, you could hire a temporary worker from one of the many placement services.

Accepting Checks

There are two distinct schools of thought regarding checks at garage sales--some say NEVER accept a check and others readily accept them. Frankly, we have never had a problem with accepting checks at any of our sales.

Not accepting checks eliminates some of your best potential customers, particularly for higher priced items. Many shoppers start out with a set amount of money and don't expect to run out during the day. By the time they get to your sale, they may be running short of cash. If there is no bank handy to cash their checks, you will not sell them much.

If you decide to accept checks, here are some common sense guidelines:

1. Accept checks only from local people written on local banks.

2. Take the customers drivers license, credit card and car license numbers. While this won't do much good if you get a bad check, just supplying the numbers implies honesty.

3. If the check is for a large amount, call the bank on which the check is written and inquire about the status of the account. While the bank will not release specific figures, they will verify that there is enough money in an account to cover a check.

4. Trust your own judgment. Most people are honest and would never think of writing a bad check. The few that do should not spoil it for the rest of us!

5. Try to obtain a list of bad check writers from one of your local merchants. Such lists are regularly updated and you may be able to obtain one that is fairly recent.

Rearranging Displays

As merchandise is sold, plan to rearrange your displays so that your display area never looks barren. It is much better to have just a few displays full of merchandise than an occasional item on tables here and there. If you have set aside any duplicates of sale items, plan to put them out as soon as the other item sells. Never let your displays get sloppy and unkempt looking.

Returns, Guarantees

For the most part, garage sales are run on the basis of WYSIWYG (What You See Is What You Get). Unless there is some compelling reason to do otherwise, treat all sales as final and do not provide any guarantees on the merchandise you sell. If you are honest with your customers as to the condition of your merchandise, no further assurances should be offered.

Signs to inform your customers of your return policy should be posted prominently. As we mentioned earlier, these could be "nasty signs" or fun signs. We prefer the latter. Try something like "ALL MERCHANDISE GUARANTEED TO THE END OF THE DRIVEWAY" or "AIN'T NOTHIN CERTAIN IN THIS LIFE, INCLUDING WHAT YOU BUY HERE!"

If a customer absolutely insists on a refund, it is better to comply than argue about it. The item in question may be in perfect condition, and the reason for the refund could be an entirely different matter. Try to be reasonable and understanding -you will gain a friend for future sales.

9

COMMON SENSE CRIME PREVENTION

Garage sales are rarely the scene of serious crimes, but shoplifting is surprisingly common. We have seen a lot of merchandise disappear at some of our sales despite our best efforts to be vigilant. Some of the folks who steal merchandise really can't afford to get it any other way, but that has rarely been the case in our experience.

You are likely to have a significant amount of cash on hand. There is always the possibility that someone will try to steal it from you. In this chapter, we will discuss some common sense ways of protecting your merchandise, your cash and (most importantly) yourself.

SALE AREA

If you are careful in setting up your sale area, some of the more common types of problems can be avoided.

Establish And Mark Boundaries

The sale area must be well defined. Boundaries should be marked. If your sale is being held in a garage or other building, the sale will be confined to that building. Outdoor displays should have their boundaries marked with ropes or fences. Other rooms or areas not included in the sale area should be marked as such. If you have provided for traffic flow as suggested earlier, controlling the boundaries of your sale should be a relatively simple matter.

> *"Opportunity makes a thief"*
> *.....Francis Bacon, 1561-1626*

Cover Your Goodies

We mentioned earlier the need to separate sale and non-sale areas and suggested that you use backgrounds for that purpose. While serving to separate the areas, backgrounds also help conceal any items not involved in the sale. If you have decided not to use backgrounds, cover expensive non-sale items with blankets or tarps during your sale. Most people have relatively valuable lawn mowers, bicycles, tools and other items stored in their garages. For anyone with criminal intent, it is easy to "case the joint" during a sale and return later to steal the valuables.

Safety In Numbers

Conducting a sale single-handedly is unwise for many reasons. For purposes of crime prevention, it is absolutely necessary that more than one person be in obvious attendance at all times. One of the most common ways of shoplifting at garage sales is for someone to distract the person in charge while accomplices steal merchandise. Having several people watching discourages this approach. Anyone with criminal intent will be reluctant to deal with a group of people--most thieves want to get in and out in a hurry without being detected.

Use Mirrors And Open Aisles

When laying out your sale, take a clue from retail stores and use wide, open aisles for shoppers to walk. Wherever possible, avoid bottlenecks and small isolated spots for someone to linger. Those areas that are difficult to see from the check out station can often be covered by a strategically placed mirror.

Plenty Of Light

One of the things shoplifters like best about garage sales is the lack of light. Many sales are held in facilities that are dimly lit. If you have followed the suggestions we made earlier, your sale will not suffer from that common problem. In addition to displaying your merchandise more effectively, light is one of the most effective deterrents to shoplifting.

Dogs Are Great

One of the best possible crime deterrents is the presence of a dog. For some reason, criminals are reluctant to take a chance with a dog present. Of course, this varies with the type of dog--a fluffy little poodle with painted nails and a bow in her hair will not strike fear in the hearts of many criminals!

Most dogs will bark in the presence of strangers, so letting your dog roam at will among shoppers would be a definite problem. The ideal solution is to tie or confine the dog out of the immediate sale area but close enough to be easily seen. If you don't have a dog, perhaps you could arrange to borrow one for the duration of your sale. If possible, choose a large hungry looking type such as a German Shepherd or Doberman Pinscher.

MERCHANDISE

Most of your garage sale merchandise will not be valuable enough to attract professional shoplifters--they will be hard at work trying to steal higher priced items from retail stores.

Amateurs, on the other hand, will steal almost anything! There are not many ways to secure ordinary garage sale merchandise from shoplifters, but your valuable items should be as secure as possible.

Valuable Items

Garage sales are not the place to try to dispose of extremely valuable items. For those items that are somewhat valuable, however, extra precautions can be taken against shoplifting:

1. Jewelry can be displayed behind glass or plastic in display cases. Alternately, you could pass a loop of wire through several jewelry pieces and securely fasten the wire to your fixture. In that way, a shopper could examine the jewelry but would need to remove the wire to steal it.

2. A wire loop or chain (a bicycle cable lock is ideal) can be passed through the button holes or hanging loops of valuable clothing items. Department stores usually reserve this type of security for leather coats, costly suits and expensive dresses.

3. Cameras or costly electronic items should be secured to a display fixture by their carrying strap or cords. Something as simple as looping the carrying strap around a table leg will prevent a shoplifter from easily walking off with a camera.

4. Put other valuables in plain sight near the check out station. Since the check out will be

staffed at all times during the sale, merchandise in that vicinity should be relatively safe.

SHOPLIFTERS

You will not see any professional shoplifters at your garage sale. Amateur shoplifters are surprisingly common. Some steal for the fun of it, others from necessity. They all steal because the opportunity is presented.

Identifying Shoplifters

While it is difficult to characterize the typical shoplifter, here are some things to watch:

1. Be suspicious of those carrying overly large purses or shopping bags. Prominent large pockets on garments or oversize coats can also be a tip-off that a shoplifter is present.

2. Most shoplifters will linger a long time in one place and spend a great deal of time watching those conducting the sale. What they are waiting for, of course, is the opportunity to slip something in a purse or pocket undetected.

3. Groups that break up when entering the sale

> *"Thieves respect property.*
> *They merely wish the property*
> *to become their property*
> *so they may more perfectly respect*
> *it."*
> *...G. K. Chesterton, 1874-1936*

area should be regarded with suspicion. Most groups of family or friends will stay together while shopping. Shoplifting groups, on the other hand, will attempt to distract your attention in one area while stealing from another.

4. While it may seem too obvious to mention, beware of those who enter the fitting room weighing 125 pounds and leave looking like they weigh 300! Any such weight gains should be immediate cause for suspicion, but be sure you don't confront anyone who started off at 300 pounds!

5. Shoppers with suspicious bulges should be viewed with some concern. As in the last item, you will want to be careful not to confront those whose bulges are a legitimate part of their anatomy!

Preventing Shoplifting

One of the best ways to prevent shoplifting is to devote a great deal of attention to those you regard as suspicious. Be friendly, look over their shoulders, ask if they need help and generally make a pest of yourself. If shoplifters realize you are not going to provide an opportunity to steal merchandise, they will leave.

If You See Someone Shoplifting

There are several possible alternatives if you suspect someone is stealing merchandise:

1. Tell them you would be happy to donate the item if they really can't afford it.

2. Charge them for the item at your check out station.

3. Ask someone else to witness the suspicious behavior in case collaboration is needed later.

4. Call the police, be sure to get a description and car license number if the shoplifter leaves.

5. Forget it and chalk the whole thing up to experience. This may be the best alternative if the merchandise involved is not really worth the effort of pursuing the shoplifter.

Check Out Area

Since the check out area will be one of the focal points of your sale, you should be able to see all around the sale area from there. Locate the check out away from displays and somewhat directly in the exit path so shoppers will have to pass by as they leave the sale area.

Watch Your Cash

One of the easiest items to steal is cash. The value is already established and cash is almost impossible to trace. Since you expect to have a relatively large amount of cash on hand, some basic precautions are in order:

1. Be sure the check out station is staffed at all times your sale is in operation.

2. Keep the cash box closed except for those times when money is actually being handled.

3. Do not let large amounts of cash build up in the cash box. Remove cash not needed to make change periodically during the sale and store that cash in a secure place.

4. Do not offer to make change for someone suspicious who asks you to break a very large bill.

5. If you accept checks, be sure to keep them in a safe place. A separate slot in the cash box will work just fine. Do not endorse checks until you are ready to cash or deposit them into your bank account. Keep a record of checks received.

6. Have a telephone at the check out station. The phone should be readily visible. Don't hesitate to use it in case of trouble.

Discretion

Criminals, like the rest of us, depend on information to make decisions. If you supply inappropriate information, the criminal may decide to act. For instance, it is foolhardy to discuss how much money you have made so far with your sale. Revealing the prices you got for expensive items, discussing quantity of goods sold or boasting about expensive collectibles, antiques or other items in your home may tempt the criminal to relieve you of some of your valuables.

Discretion also applies to items outside the sale area. **Do not let anyone wander outside the sale area for any reason.** As we mentioned earlier, cover any valuables that are not included in the sale.

IN CASE OF TROUBLE

While it is extremely rare, you may encounter an actual hold-up situation. Most often, criminals do not actually carry a weapon, but indicate the presence of one. If this should happen to you, DO NOT try to be a hero. Here are some suggestions:

1. Hand over the cash box or whatever it is that the criminal wants.

2. Be observant. Concentrate on trying to develop a description of the criminal. Height, weight, clothing, identifying features and peculiarities are all things that will help the authorities .

3. Do not confront shoplifters or minor league criminals yourself. Use the telephone to call for help. No garage sale merchandise is worth the risk of a possible confrontation.

4. Although it sounds trite, try to stay as calm as possible!

CLOSING THE SALE

Just as every garage sale has a beginning, it must also have an end. When the advertised closing time has passed and customers have stopped coming, the end has been reached. Although you may want to continue the sale a little longer if there are people shopping at closing time, there is no sense waiting around in hopes that a few stragglers may happen by.

If you have had a successful sale, there will not be much merchandise left and many things to do before you can call it a day. If you have had an offer to buy out the remaining inventory, this is the time to contact the buyer and make arrangements for the transaction.

Advertising And Signs

As soon as your sale is closed, remove ALL the signs and posters you have in place. Start with the signs on major traffic arteries and work backward toward your sale location. There is nothing more irritating to a shopper than following signs to a sale that was held last week! Unless you want some unwelcome visitors at your house, be sure to remove all your signs as soon as possible after the sale. If you have kept a list of places your signs and posters are located, removal should be a relatively simple (but important) process.

If you are careful removing and storing your signs, they can be used again. The dates may have to be changed, but that is much easier than making all new signs. Perhaps one of your customers has read this book and will offer to buy all your signs.

One thing frequently overlooked--post a **"Sale Closed"** sign at your location. This will eliminate potential shoppers scouring your neighborhood looking for a sale that is already closed.

Count Your Cash

At the conclusion of your sale, count your cash and checks and then remove them to some safe place. If you have sold merchandise for others, are dividing advertising costs or have made other financial arrangements, be sure to provide both the cash and records punctually. Usually this is done within a day or so of the sale, after you have had a chance to clean up the sale area. A count of the total cash receipts at the end of the sale is the starting point for any division and should be done as soon as possible.

Consigned Merchandise

Any merchandise consigned to your sale should be promptly returned to its owner or paid for. You should supply a list of what was sold and the price obtained for each item unless the consignment consisted largely of small, low priced items. If you made arrangements with the consignors to pick up merchandise at the conclusion of the sale, be sure to have everything ready for them.

Unsold Items

If your sale has been successful, you will be left with relatively few items. It is very rare, however, to sell everything. Most of us are left with some merchandise and must decide how best to get rid of it. Here are some possibilities:

1. Store merchandise until your next garage sale. If the items are not bulky and storage is no problem, this idea has some merit.

2. Place unsold items in someone else's sale. This approach has worked for us several times. We have changed the price or done something to enhance the salability of each item and sold it at another sale.

3. Worthy causes are always looking for used merchandise. In our area the Salvation Army and Goodwill will pick up unsold items and put them to good use.

4. Sell the entire stock to a professional flea or resale shop. Although their prices are not usually what you would like to get, this is one way to clear out your remaining stock.

5. Craft items can be sold at some other type of sale such as a craft sale or church bazaar. If the items are non-perishable, it is a good idea to try to sell them at another time.

6. Baked goods or perishable items must be used before they spoil. If your family doesn't like baked goods, they may be donated to a local shelter or senior center. You might consider giving some of the baked goods to your neighbors as compensation for any inconvenience they experienced during your

sale (otherwise known as greasing the wheels for your next sale!) Any remaining items can be frozen for use at some later time.

CRITIQUE

One of the most valuable things you can do immediately after a sale is to sit down and write a critique of the sale. While everything is fresh in your mind, record your observations in several areas:

1. Advertising--what was most effective? Which customers mentioned advertising in particular? Did you sell special items that were heavily advertised? How did most shoppers find out about your sale? Were shoppers waiting for your sale to open?

2. Physical arrangements--which displays were most effective? Did customers complain or compliment you on anything? Did you provide well enough for weather and other contingencies? How was parking and how could it have been improved?

3. Price levels for various types of merchandise. Jot down both the asking and actual selling prices. Was any of your merchandise under priced? Overpriced? What kinds of comments did you hear about your prices?

> *"Experience is the name*
> *everyone gives*
> *to their mistakes"*
> *.....Oscar Wilde 1854-1900*

4. What items did not sell? Why not? Did they sell after you changed prices or display techniques? Was there a demand for the items you offered for sale?

5. What kinds of items did your customers request? Where could you get some of those items for your next sale? What kinds of prices do you think your customers would be willing to pay for those items?

6. How could you improve future sales? Jot down ideas in the areas of advertising, organization, merchandising techniques, special arrangements or sources of display fixtures. List those items you found to be particularly ineffective along with those that were successful.

GARAGE SALES AS A BUSINESS

One of the first questions you may ask yourself after a successful sale is, "Am I interested in doing this again?" Often the answer is a qualified "Yes." Yes, if I can find enough merchandise at the right price. Yes, if I have enough space to store the merchandise until the next sale. Yes, if I can sell my merchandise at a profit. Yes, if my neighbors will tolerate a sale again in the near future. Yes, if I can find enough help to run the sale.

Some people have a sale only once in a lifetime,

> *"Hindsight is always
> twenty-twenty."*
> *...Billy Wilder, 1906--*

others nearly every weekend. More frequent sales require considerably more effort, but have the potential of producing significantly more profit. As you conduct more and more sales, you may decide to become a "Full time junker" or "Professional Flea."

Advantages

There are many advantages to becoming a garage sale entrepreneur:

1. You can be your own boss.

2. If you are a perceptive shopper of other sales, you will have a relatively small investment in inventory. The secret to inventory is, of course, to buy low and sell at a profit.

3. Since this is basically a work at home type of business, you will enjoy flexible hours.

4. Garage sales can be an excellent source of income IF you follow the steps outlined in this book, have a good location and are extremely careful about the merchandise you buy.

5. You will already have signs, display fixtures and other items needed for your first sale--they will serve you just as well for subsequent sales.

> *"There are few ways in which a man can be more innocently employed than in getting money"*
> *.....Samuel Johnson, 1709-1874*

Disadvantages

Along with advantages, of course, come disadvantages:

1. In order to be a successful garage sale entrepreneur, you must have a good selection of merchandise. This will involve running around to a lot of other sales and buying things at distressed prices.

2. You will need to sharpen your bargaining skills and use them often.

3. Once you have purchased items to resell, they must be cleaned, repaired, priced and stored until your next sale. If you have a lot of extra storage space, this is no problem.

4. It is possible, of course, that you may be stuck with a lot of junk. (Isn't that the reason you had your first sale?)

5. Shoppers tend to shy away from professional sales since they feel the prices reflect a mark-up from what they could buy items for themselves.

6. Consider your neighbors, since frequent sales may raise problems that are not likely to surface with once or twice a year garage sales.

Other Considerations

Although they are not necessarily advantages or disadvantages, here are some things to consider before deciding to make a business of garage sales:

1. Cities often limit the number of sales you can hold without a permit, sales tax and resale license.

2. A professional operation will need liability insurance since your homeowners policy will probably will not cover more than an occasional sale.

3. Zoning restrictions and covenants limit the number or type of sales that may be held on your property.

An Alternative

If you are a proficient garage sale organizer and conductor, why not sell your services to others? You can work for a fixed fee or percentage of the total sales.   Other people will supply the merchandise, sale location, advertising budget and clean-up crew.

Most professional sale organizers get involved with merchandise selection, pricing, advertising and promotional efforts, conducting the sale and dividing up the profits. Since they are supplying expertise which will increase profits, a fee of 10 to 20% of total sales is not unreasonable.

If you decide to go this route, be prepared to

> *"Nothing great was ever achieved*
> *without enthusiasm"*
> *.....R. W. Emerson, 1803-1882*

give each sale a maximum effort and leave each customer feeling as though your fee was a bargain. You'll soon have more business than you can handle, strictly from word of mouth. Don't neglect other promotional efforts, however. Advertise your services in the Garage Sale classifieds, hand out business cards at your own and other sales and get the word out that you're available.

Most of the sales we will be discussing in this chapter are similar to garage sales in their basic design and execution. There are, however, important enough differences for them to merit our special attention.

SPECIALTY GOODS

Some specialized types of goods lend themselves well to separate sales. Among these are sports cards and memorabilia, coins, comic books, records, tools, firearms, auto parts and accessories, antiques, glassware and collectors items.

Definition

Specialty goods can be defined as those items which attract significant attention on their own. Usually this is in the form of enthusiasts or collectors, although some types of specialty goods may appeal to the general public.

Seasons

Merchandise which is season sensitive will sell best just before or in the early part of its' prime use season. If you have a significant amount of specialized merchandise to sell, you may well consider holding your sale during the off season for other types of sales. This will insure an interested audience, since the range of sales from which to choose will be relatively slim.

Target Your Advertising

If you hope to attract those interested in specialty items, you must know how to reach them. Newspaper classified ads will reach people interested in just about anything, but other types of advertising will definitely be needed to reach specific groups of people.

One of the best ways to reach enthusiasts in just about any area is to contact some of the many clubs that publish newsletters. A check of your local newsstand will usually reveal at least a magazine or newsletter devoted to the specialty items you have for sale. Advertising in these publications is effective in reaching other enthusiasts. Don't confine your search to just your immediate area, since people will often travel significant distances to attend a large sale. Advertise early enough so the folks you hope to attract have time to put your sale on their schedule.

Be Knowledgeable

The best chance for a successful specialty sale comes with knowledge about the merchandise you are trying to sell and the people to whom it will appeal:

1. Know which pieces are valuable and which aren't.

2. Know what to target in your advertising to attract the largest possible crowd.

3. Know what each item does, what kind of condition it's in and what is a fair price.

4, Know enough about the merchandise so you can talk intelligently about it and be able to answer questions for beginners.

This is not to say that you must necessarily possess all the expertise called for in this section. It is usually possible to find a few other people with similar interests who would be glad to help with your sale and provide a broader base of knowledge. As a matter of fact, they may be interested in selling some of their own merchandise or buying some of yours!

Price References

For most types of specialty merchandise, there are published price references available. While these references may not reflect the prices you will be able to get, at least they will provide a starting point for both setting prices and later negotiation. Usually price reference manuals provide some additional information about the merchandise that may prove very valuable during your sale.

You must be careful, however, that you do not appear too knowledgeable. Most collectors and enthusiasts shop sales where they feel it is possible to get a good bargain. If you deliberately slightly under price some of your merchandise, you can be sure they will linger long enough to check out everything in your sale.

Setting Up Your Sale

Consider the type of merchandise you will be offering and the prices you expect to charge when setting up your sale. You cannot sell valuable antiques in the same way you sell garage sale merchandise. There is an old adage that says "You have to spend money to make money"--this is particularly true when your prime concentration will be on relatively large ticket items. Provide a well planned shopping area and be sure to include some nice refreshments. Treat your customers well and they will respond to your efforts by buying merchandise.

ESTATE SALES

Estate sales are garage sales with difficult emotions attached. Usually there is some emotional attachment to the merchandise. Emotions are often strained, particularly if the loss is recent. While most garage sales are relatively happy occasions, estate sales represent a finality that many people find disturbing.

Differences

Garage sales feature selected merchandise, often from several individuals or families. Estate sales typically consist of all the left-over possessions of an individual or family. Prime items may have been divided among the heirs and the remaining household goods are left for the estate sale. There is usually little agreement as to how the remaining possessions and proceeds from the estate sale will be divided. While garage sales are organized as primarily money making operations, estate sales are often geared toward getting rid of the merchandise at any cost.

Sale Items

In most estate sales, there is a good variety of items. If you are charged with setting up the sale, you should first go through everything and discard those items which are unsuitable for any reason. Personal hygiene, worn-out garments, family keepsakes and "spoken for" items should be excluded from the sale. All items to be included in the sale must be sorted, cleaned, grouped and priced. Setting up displays should follow the principles we have outlined earlier. Be especially careful not to clutter up the displays so badly that individual items cannot be readily seen.

Location

When considering the location for an estate sale, remember that merchandise can be sold in place or moved to another location. It may be easiest to sell everything in place, unless that presents an emotional problem for you. If you decide to move everything to another location, be sure to consider all the location factors we mentioned earlier. It is especially important that you choose the location with the best possible traffic flow, since most estate sales are relatively short.

Pricing

Since there are often several people involved in the disposition of an estate, setting prices may have to be done in a group. This is often easier said than done! Getting everyone to agree on prices takes considerable negotiating skill. Perhaps the best approach is to get everyone to agree on a third party who will come in and set prices on all the merchandise. You can save yourself a lot of time and grief using the third party approach!

Advertising

Mention the fact that this will be an estate sale in your advertising. If your newspaper offers classifications for both estate and garage sales, list yours in both places. Describe the best items in both ads. If there is too much merchandise to list, consider listing general groups (antique furniture, men and women's clothing, comic book collection, etc.).   Use the same advertising techniques we mentioned earlier in this book.

Stay Away "If"

Estate sales involve a whole different range of emotions than garage sales. If you find it difficult to see some things sold or you are too emotional from your recent loss, consider having someone else run the sale for you. Stay away until the sale is finished and leave it to whoever is in charge to dispose of the inventory in any way possible.

Consider An Auction

Auctions are often used to dispose of the contents of an estate, including some relatively major items such as real estate and automobiles. You may wish to consider an auction instead of an estate sale under the following conditions:

1. It is too emotionally difficult for you to dispose of the estate items.

2. All the people involved cannot agree on what to sell and what prices to charge.

3. You feel the job is simply too overwhelming to tackle alone.

4. You need professional help to sort, arrange and dispose of the contents of the estate.

5. You cannot devote the time necessary to conduct the sale yourself.

CRAFT SALES

Group craft sales are often scheduled to coincide with the prime time for major holiday shopping. There are many advantages to group sales, but those with a good selection of distinctive merchandise may do as well on their own.

Merchandise

If you have a limited variety of merchandise, a group sale may be just what you need. Keep in mind, however, there may be many people with similar merchandise. If you have a good selection of crafts to offer, an individual sale will provide you with an opportunity to showcase your talents. Your efforts will be more appreciated with an individual sale, but there is a lot of work involved in putting on a successful craft sale.

Prices

In a group situation, your prices must be competitive with other sellers. If they offer similar merchandise at a lower price than yours, chances are they'll sell more than you. Prices at an individual sale can be less restricted, although you should be somewhat competitive with other craft people in your area.

Display

The way you display craft items must be in keeping with the nature of the merchandise. Displays must reflect quality and originality. Dare to be different--use fancier fixtures, more light, unusual materials, etc. Make your merchandise stand out from the crowd. Offer gift boxes or wrapping for the holidays. Customize any items that lend themselves well to that approach. Make it easy for shoppers to buy!

The most common problem with craft displays is simply piling up too much merchandise. It really doesn't matter to the shopper that you have made 500 wooden rabbits--he is interested in only one. That one rabbit, creatively and attractively displayed, will sell much faster than one in a large pile of similar rabbits. **If you have a quantity of items that are the same, display only a few at a time and restock your displays when some sell.** This one idea will net you considerably more sales than any other we offer in this section!

Have plenty of light for your display area. Use gooseneck lights, clamping lamps, desk lamps, self-sticking fixtures or whatever else it takes to show your merchandise to best advantage.

Advertising

The amount of advertising you need depends on the format of your sale. If this is to be a large group sale, chances are the advertising costs will be built into the participation fee. Most advertising for large group sales is institutional in nature and merely promotes the sale itself. Rarely are individual participants mentioned. Smaller group sales are more individualized.

If you are conducting a craft sale on your own, advertising is critical to attracting shoppers. You must be specific, interesting, and creative. Describe your merchandise in such a way as to create demand on the part of potential shoppers. All of the advertising principles we discussed earlier apply to craft sales, whether individual or group efforts.

"WORTHY CAUSE" SALES

Charitable groups have discovered there is money to be made selling merchandise people want to buy at prices they want to pay. This secret has long been known to the retail world and has made for many successful careers. Charitable groups have a distinct advantage when it comes to sales in that they rarely pay for much of their inventory! Most things are donated, so the selling price is primarily profit. Those who donate goods feel as though they are helping and shoppers are often willing to pay a little more for items when they feel the proceeds are going to help some worthy cause.

Merchandise

The range of merchandise to be found at "worthy cause" sales is wide indeed. Generally, however, things tend to fall into one of three general categories:

1. Baked goods, often donated by members of the group. There is also a definite market for ready to bake goods. Most bake sales run for only a day and need a great deal of advance publicity. Creating a demand on the part of shoppers is relatively easy, since not many people bake anymore. With the large number of working couples, baking at home has suffered considerably. Fortunately, many folks love the taste of homebaked goods and are willing to pay the price to buy it.

If your group decides to try an "unbake" sale, plan ahead and take as many advance orders as possible. Unbaked goods are perishable and should be either baked or frozen within a short period of time. Once frozen, things keep quite well and can be used at a later time.

2. Specialty goods are specific categories of items to which members of your group have access. For example, our local Friends of The Library group sponsors a couple of used book and magazine sales during the year. Some of the merchandise is from the library, much of it is donated by bookstores and individuals. It is surprising how much money can be raised by selling books and magazines at almost give away prices.

   Your group might decide to have a record sale, book fair, baseball card swap meet, used sporting goods exchange, computer software sale or kids toy sale. As long as the merchandise appeals to enough people, the sale will be a success.

3. Garage sale is the most popular and least successful type of group sale. Participants tend to donate merchandise which cannot be disposed of in any other way (a nice way of saying garbage!) and avid garage sale shoppers avoid group sales because of low quality merchandise and high prices.

   Your group can hold a successful garage sale, but there are many misperceptions you must overcome. If your sales in the past have been successful, don't change the format you have been following. It takes several years for a sale to gain a good reputation, so don't be discouraged if your first effort is less successful than you would like it to be.

Advertising

As we've said numerous times throughout this book--**Advertising is critical to the success of any sale**. If your group intends to raise a significant amount of money from any type of sale, there must be sufficient advertising to attract shoppers. There are advantages to working with a group in that many people can spread the word much more effectively than just a few. In addition to strong word of mouth, be sure to allocate enough money for commercial advertising and use it to good advantage!

Appendix A.
Checklists

Well In Advance Of The Sale

❑ Shop other sales in the area to:

  ❑ Gather ideas.

  ❑ Buy bargain priced merchandise to resell.

  ❑ Accumulate specialty merchandise (i.e., toys, baby goods) if you have decided to have that type of sale.

❑ Set sale date.

  ❑ Check community schedule for possible conflicts.

  ❑ Decide if you want prime season sale or off season event.

❑ Sale location.

  ❑ If possible, choose best location for traffic flow and adequate space.

  ❑ Prepare tentative layout.

  ❑ Set timetable for general cleaning and preparation of sale area.

  ❑ Check with your neighbors, set up a parking plan.

❑ Merchandise.

- ❑ Select merchandise of your own.

- ❑ Clean, repair and package all merchandise.

- ❑ Prepare any special items (plants, crafts, etc.).

❑ Purchase Supplies

- ❑ Send for Silver Streak's Catalog of Garage Sale Supplies..

- ❑ Material for signs.

- ❑ Tags and labels for merchandise.

- ❑ Extension cords.

- ❑ Material for backgrounds.

- ❑ Bags and boxes to carry merchandise.

❑ Advertising.

- ❑ Prepare handout for neighbors and friends informing them of sale and inviting them to participate.

- ❑ Prepare schedule for ordering and placing newspaper ads.

- ❑ Select tentative locations for signs.

- ❑ Prepare list of signs needed.

- ❑ Arrange for posters to be made.

❑ Miscellaneous.

     ❑ Check with city and county officials to see if permits are needed.

     ❑ Be sure your homeowner's liability insurance covers garage sales.

     ❑ Check rental shops for available fixtures, signs, etc.

The Week Prior To Your Sale.

❑ Sale area.

     ❑ Final cleaning of the entire area.

     ❑ Prepare final layout and traffic flow diagram.

     ❑ Arrange for rental or borrowed fixtures.

     ❑ Assemble and place all display fixtures.

     ❑ Try and, if necessary, revise layout with fixtures in place.

     ❑ Arrange lighting and try to be sure everything works as planned.

     ❑ Set up backgrounds to cover non-sale items.

     ❑ Arrange for any fans or heaters likely to be needed.

❑ Set up check out area.

❑ Merchandise.

    ❑ Clean, repair and hang all clothes. Mark with size and price.

    ❑ Clean, polish and repair all other merchandise.

    ❑ Replace batteries in those items needing them.

    ❑ Arrange for consignment items to be delivered in time to set up your displays.

    ❑ Arrange for baked (or unbaked) goods to be available on time.

❑ Advertising.

    ❑ Place newspaper advertisements.

    ❑ Finish making all your signs and posters.

    ❑ Distribute sale handouts to friends, relatives, etc.

    ❑ Post sale notices on local bulletin boards.

    ❑ Make final arrangements for sign placement sites.

❑ Miscellaneous

❏ Purchase a pad of receipts.

❏ Secure a list of bad check writers from a
   local merchant.

❏ Order refreshments.

❏ Set up a schedule for helpers.

One Day Prior To The Sale.

❏ Sale Area.

   ❏ Make any last minute arrangement
      changes.

   ❏ Dust and spot clean any areas where
      needed.

   ❏ Test lights, electrical cords and music
      system.

   ❏ Post any necessary indoor signs in their
      proper places.

   ❏ Place fans or heaters as needed.

   ❏ Pick up any rental fixtures.

   ❏ Have display area ready for baked goods,
      refreshments.

❏ Merchandise.

   ❏ Add final merchandise to displays.

- ❑ Check to see everything is marked with price, size, etc.

- ❑ Have merchandise ready to move outdoors if you plan to do so.

❑ Check Out Area.

- ❑ Get coins and currency for cash box.

- ❑ Place boxes, bags, etc. at the check out.

- ❑ Check to be sure that you can see all around the sale area.

- ❑ Place phone at check out.

- ❑ Have receipts and note pads on hand.

- ❑ Have a tape measure or yardstick available.

❑ Advertising.

- ❑ Deliver handouts describing your sale to others in the area.

- ❑ Pick up handouts to give away at your sale.

- ❑ Pick up any rental items such as sign boards, lights, etc.

❑ Personnel.

- ❑ Confirm schedules of those who will be helping with the sale.

❏ Prepare a place for the dog.

❏ Set time for consignors to pick up their merchandise.

Day Of Sale

❏ Advertising.

  ❏ Place signs at predetermined locations, starting farthest away.

  ❏ Mark parking areas, including a loading zone.

  ❏ Remove your own vehicles from the sale area.

  ❏ Set up the entrance signs, banners, balloons, etc.

❏ Sale area.

  ❏ Prepare and place refreshments.

  ❏ Lights, fans, music and appliances operating.

  ❏ Baked goods and perishables in place.

  ❏ Cash box ready to be placed at the check out station.

  ❏ Dog in place.

❏ Miscellaneous.

- ❏ Open your sale on time.

- ❏ Relax and enjoy the sale!

❏ Closing time.

- ❏ Close the entrance and exit to the sale area.

- ❏ Post "Sale Closed" sign at the entrance.

- ❏ If this is the final day, remove all your signs. (Check your list to be sure you have them all).

- ❏ Remove the cash box to a safe location.

After The Sale.

❏ Cash Box

- ❏ Count your cash and checks.

- ❏ Deposit the checks.

- ❏ Divide the proceeds if you had multiple sellers.

❏ Remaining merchandise.

- ❏ Donate to charity if unwanted.

- ❏ Return to owners if consigned.

- ❏ Box up and store for your next sale if you have storage room.

❑ Dump in the trash if no charity will accept it.

❑ Advertising.

   ❑ Be sure all your signs have been removed carefully) and stored.

   ❑ Take down posters and flyers posted around town.

   ❑ Return unused flyers for other sales if they are in the future.

❑ Sale area.

   ❑ Dismantle the fixtures, return any borrowed or rented units.

   ❑ Return sale area to its original (if somewhat cleaner) condition.

❑ **BEGIN PLANNING YOUR NEXT SALE!**

Appendix B.
Signs And Samples

In this section, there are a few ideas for signs and other promotional materials. Our ideas can be adapted to your particular situation. We hope something you see here will help make your sale more profitable.

Creative signs are crucial   to the overall success of your sale. Since signs will be one of your primary advertising mediums, be willing to spend the time and money necessary to make them as effective as possible. Hopefully, the ideas presented in the last few pages will give you some ideas for your own signs.

Letters can be an effective advertising tool when sent to people you know would be interested in some of the merchandise at your sale. Here are a couple of possibilities:

Dear Bill & Nancy,

We will be hosting a Garage Sale at our house on Thursday, Friday and Saturday, June 20, 21 and 22. I know you are interested in collecting ceramics and early American art, so you will be especially excited about some of the items we will be offering.

Our sale will begin at 8:00 AM on the 20th, but we will be serving coffee and donuts for our friends at 7:00. Hope to see you then!

Sincerely,

John Jones

Dear Gail,

I have heard many positive comments regarding the natural childbirth classes you are teaching.

We are preparing to host a Garage Sale at our house that might be of great interest to the students in your classes. The majority of our merchandise will be for babies! In cooperation with some of our friends, we have assembled a large collection of everything new parents will need for their baby. We have cribs, car seats, clothing, toys, scales, strollers and hundreds of other items.

We would like your class to have first chance at the best items, so we will open the sale just for them at 7:00 AM on Thursday, June 20th. Free coffee and donuts will be served.

Our sale will run Thursday, Friday and Saturday, June 20, 21 and 22 from 8:00 AM to 5:00 PM. Our address is 1910 Elm Street.

Looking forward to seeing you again!

Jane Jones

In addition to letters to special friends, flyers can help announce your sale to the rest of your friends and neighbors. On the next two pages there are samples of flyers that can be adapted to almost any type of sale.

NEIGHBORHOOD GARAGE
SALE
THURS., FRI., SAT.
JUNE 20, 21, 22.

YOU ARE CORDIALLY INVITED
TO
PARTICIPATE.

PLANNING MEETING MON.,
MAY 12
7:00

THE SMITH'S
1910 ELM STREET
555-1234

WE'RE HAVING A GARAGE
SALE:

JIM AND MARY SMITH
1910 ELM STREET
555-1234

THE SALE WILL BE HELD
THURSDAY,
FRIDAY & SATURDAY
JUNE 20, 21, 22.

IF YOU WOULD LIKE TO
CONSIGN MERCHANDISE OR
HELP WITH THE SALE,
PLEASE CONTACT US!

THANKS.

GIGANTIC GARAGE SALE

THURS., FRI. & SAT
JUNE 20, 21, 22
8:00 TO 4:30

1910 ELM STREET

FEATURING:

ANTIQUE FURNITURE
CHILDREN'S TOYS
BOYS CLOTHES, SIZES 6-12
BABY CLOTHES
LADIES SIZE 10-14
MEN'S WORK CLOTHES
LAWN MOWER
POWER TOOLS
PLANTS
MISCELLANY GALORE!!

SPECIAL PREVIEW
THURSDAY, JUNE 20
6:00 TO 8:00 AM
FREE COFFEE AND DONUTS

Appendix C.
Pricing Guides And
Sources Of Information

Many books, magazines and even videotapes are available to help with your garage sale and some of the special merchandise you may be interested in selling. This list is not meant to be all inclusive, but rather to give you a place to start looking for further information. Consult your library and bookstore for more possibilities.

Angus, S. F. Collecting Antiques. New York: Galahad Books, 1974.

Beck, Doreen. Collecting Country & Western Americana. New York: Crown Publishers, 1975.

Beitler, Arline. Adventures of a Cheap Antiquer. New York: Avon, 1979.

Brunner, Marguerite Ashworth. Antiques For Amateurs On A Shoestring Budget. Indianapolis, IN: Bobbs-Merrill, 1976.

Bunn, Eleanore. Metal Molds: ice cream, chocolate, barley. Paducah, KY: Collector Books, 1981.

Callahan, Claire (Wallis). How To Sell Your Antiques At A Profit. New York: D. McKay Co., 1969.

Cowie, Donald. Antiques: how to identify and collect them. South Brunswick: A. S. Barnes, 1971.

DeWein, S. and Ashabraner, J. The Collectors Encyclopedia of Barbie Dolls And Collectibles.

Paducah, KY: Collector Books (P.O. Box 3009, Paducah, KY 42002-3009)

Farwell, William H. What Is It Worth? : Advice on buying and selling antiques. Rutland, VT: C.E. Tuttle Co., 1973.

Feinman, Jeffrey. Collecting Tomorrow's Collectibles. New York: Collier Books, 1979.

Flayderman, Norm. Collecting Tomorrow's Antiques Today. Garden City, NY: Doubleday, 1972.

Gohm, Douglas. Small Antiques For The Collector. New York: Arco, 1970.

Groberman, Jeff. The Garage Sale Book. Rocklin, CA: Prima Publishing and Communications, 1987.

Grotz, George. Grotz's Decorative Collectibles Price Guide. Garden City, NY: Dolphin Books, Doubleday, 1983.

Hastin, Bud. Bud Hastins Avon Bottle Encyclopedia: the official Avon collector's guide. Ft. Lauderdale, FL (P.O. Box 8400, Fort Lauderdale 33310): B. Hastin, 1981.

Hothem, Lar. Collecting Farm Antiques. Florence, AL: Books Americana, 1982.

House of Collectibles. The Official Identification and Price Guide to Antiques and

Collectibles, 10th ed. Orlando, FL: House of Collectibles, 1989.

House of Collectibles. The Official Price Guide to Antiques and Collectibles. Orlando, FL: House of Collectibles, 1987.

House of Collectibles. The Official Price Guide to Paper Collectibles. Orlando, FL: House of Collectibles, 1984.

How To Have A Moneymaking Garage Sale. (videocassette)   Los   Angeles,   CA: J2 Communications, 1987.

Hudson, William N. Antiques At Auction. South Brunswick: A.S. Barnes, 1972.

Jenkins, Emyl. Emyl Jenkins Appraisal Book. Crown Publishers, 1989.

Jenkins, Emyl. Emyl Jenkins Guide to Buying and Collecting Early American Furniture. Crown Publishers, 1991.

Ketchum, William C. The Catalog of American Collectibles. New York: Mayflower Books, 1979.

Kovel, Ralph. Kovel's Know Your Antiques, revised & updated. New York: Crown, 1990.

Kovel, Ralph. Kovel's Know Your Collectibles. New York: Crown, 1981.

Lewis, Mel. How To Make Money From Antiques. Poole, (England): Blandford Press, 1981.

Mackay, James. Antiques of The Future: A guide for collectors. New York: Universe Books, 1970.

Madigan, Mary Jean. Americana, folk and decorative art. New York: Art & Antiques, 1982.

Manos, Paris and Susan. The Wonder of Barbie Dolls And Accessories 1976-1986. Paducah, KY: Collector Books.

Mebane, John. What's New That's Old: offbeat collectibles. South Brunswick, NJ: A.S. Barnes, 1970.

Petty, Ryan. How To Make More Money With Your Garage Sale. New York: St. Martin's Press, 1981.

Pohl, Irma. Rummage, Tag & Garage Sales: nine easy steps to turn rummage into cash. Garden City, NY: Mary Ellen Family Books/Doubleday, 1984.

Rothschild, Sigmund. A Beginner's Guide To Antiques and Collectibles. New York: Pharos books, 1989.

Salter, Stefan. Joys of Hunting Antiques. New York: Hart Publishing Co., 1971.

Stevenson, Chris. Garage Sale Mania: How to hold a profitable garage, yard or tag sale. White Hall, VA: Betterway Publications, 1988.

Time-Life Books. The Encyclopedia of Collectibles. Alexandria, VA: Time-Life Books, 1978-1980.

Ullman, James. How to Hold a Garage Sale. Chicago: Rand McNally, 1981.

Warman's Americana & Collectibles. Elkins Park, PA: Warman Publishing Company, 1984.

Young, Jean. The Better Garage Sale Book. New York: Bantam, 1974.

PLEASE SHARE

We'd like to hear about your Garage Sale ideas and experiences. We may include them in a future edition of this book. If yours are used, we'll send you a copy of the book <u>free of charge</u>! Thank you for sharing.

Use this page, or if you'd rather not mutilate your copy of this book, send a separate sheet to:

Silver Streak Publications
1823 Sussex Ct.
Bettendorf, IA 52722-3156

Phone or FAX (319) 355-3341

Order Blank

If you are unable to locate them at your local bookstore, you may use this order blank to obtain additional copies of "The Backyard Money Machine" or to obtain information on the other products from Silver Streak Publications.

Please Send:

___ Copies of "The Backyard Money Machine"

@$9.95 :_____

___ Catalog of other Silver Streak products.(free)

Shipping:
Book Rate:$1.75 for the first book, .75 for each additional book. Air mail: $3.00 per book.

Sales Tax:
Iowa residents add 6% sales tax.

Make check payable to Silver Streak Publications.

Mail to:

Silver Streak Publications
1823 Sussex Court
Bettendorf, IA 52722-3156

Thank You!